The Trial of Elizabeth Gurley Flynn by the American Civil Liberties Union

Edited by Corliss Lamont

Preface by Maxwell Geismar

Modern Reader Paperbacks
New York and London

To the Memory of
DR. HARRY F. WARD,
Chairman, 1920–1940, Board of Directors
of the American Civil Liberties Union

Copyright © 1968 by Corliss Lamont
All Rights Reserved
Library of Congress Catalog Card Number: 79-91313
First Modern Reader Paperback Edition 1969 AUG 12 '71
First Printing

Published by Monthly Review Press
116 West 14th Street, New York, N. Y. 10011
33/37 Moreland Street, London, E.C. 4

Originally published in 1968 by
Horizon Press

Manufactured in the United States of America

CONTENTS

Page 7   *Preface by Maxwell Geismar*

13   Introduction

31   *A.C.L.U. Board Members Present at Trial*

35   Part I   Transcript of the Trial
The Board of Directors of the American Civil Liberties Union hears the three formal charges for the expulsion of Elizabeth Gurley Flynn from the Board. The A.C.L.U. Resolution of February 5, 1940, proscribing certain opinions for Union's officers and staff. Miss Flynn starts to read defense statement. Discussion and vote as to whether certain letters are to be received in evidence

Trial Exhibit:
44   A.C.L.U. Resolution of February 5, 1940

99   Part II   The Transcript Continued
The Board discusses first charge, as to whether Elizabeth Gurley Flynn's membership in the Communist Party is inconsistent with Resolution of February 5, 1940, and whether such membership precludes her from functioning properly as a Director of the Civil Liberties Union. Miss Flynn concludes reading of defense.

51176

She replies to direct questioning by various members of the Board. At Chairman's request Miss Flynn retires from meeting. Discussion on second and third charges. The Board votes on the three charges without recalling Miss Flynn

Trial Exhibits:

Page 145   Letter from Roger W. Riis to Dr. John Haynes Holmes, March 17, 1940

147   Article, "Your World and Mine," by Norman Thomas in Socialist *Call*, December 16, 1939

153   Article, "I Am Expelled from Civil Liberties," by Elizabeth Gurley Flynn in *Sunday Worker*, March 17, 1940

157   Article, "Why I Won't Resign from the A.C.L.U.," by Elizabeth Gurley Flynn in *New Masses*, March 19, 1940

165   Letter from B. W. Huebsch to the Directors of the A.C.L.U., April 19, 1940

193   Constitution and By-Laws of Communist Party, U.S.A.

Part III   Appendices

183   Appendix One: *Why We Defend Free Speech for Nazis, Fascists and Communists—An Answer to Critics Who Would Deny Liberty to Those They Characterize as Enemies of Democracy*, by the Board of Directors of the American Civil Liberties Union, April, 1939

187   Appendix Two: "A Statement to Members and Friends of the American Civil Liberties Union," released to the press by the A.C.L.U. on February 5, 1940

4

Page 189   Appendix Three: Open Letter to the A.C.L.U. from Seventeen Liberals, March 18, 1940

193   Appendix Four: Constitution and By-Laws of the Communist Party of the United States of America

211   Appendix Five: Letter of Resignation, March 2, 1940, from Dr. Harry F. Ward, Chairman of A.C.L.U. Board of Directors, 1920–1940

214   Appendix Six: Protest to the A.C.L.U. National Committee and Board of Directors by Three Members of the National Committee, March 21, 1940

218   Appendix Seven: Protest by A. F. Whitney, President of the Brotherhood of Railroad Trainmen and Member of the National Committee of the A.C.L.U., August 18, 1940

224   Appendix Eight: Vote of the National Committee of the A.C.L.U. ratifying the expulsion of Elizabeth Gurley Flynn

PREFACE

by Maxwell Geismar

In future history books written by Asian and African scribes, it may be recorded that the period of the 1960's in the Free White World was marked by a brief resurgence of the old-fashioned American spirit in a general epoch of censorship, conformity, and repression. During this unique and short-lived period, there flourished a considerable body of Cold War revisionist historians, from the first generation of D. F. Fleming, Frederick Schuman, and William Appleman Williams to such brilliant young critics as David Horowitz and Gar Alperovitz, and many others now on our horizon.

But, alas, their work has never been taken seriously by the majority of cultivated and prosperous Americans who lived out a spiritual existence dominated by the horrendous Cold War myths of the 1950's and 1960's. To them the Rosenbergs were forever guilty and Alger Hiss remained the classic example of *their* betrayal. I doubt that even such a book as Corliss Lamont's *The Trial of Elizabeth Gurley Flynn*, which also includes the transcript of the "extraordinary meeting" of the Board of Directors of the American Civil Liberties Union —a transcript of which a large part has been expunged from the official records of the A.C.L.U.—will have the impact it should have on the national consciousness. But that should not diminish interest in reading a book which gets at the core of our moral dissolution during the Cold War period.

Fortunately for history, Corliss Lamont had a copy of the complete transcript of the Flynn "trial" by the A.C.L.U. Board. One of the interesting things is that the Board itself could never decide whether it was a trial, a hearing, a friendly or hostile discussion, or a gathering of curious soul-mates some of whom were out to get the others. But whatever it was supposed to be, this transcript remains a historical document full of illumination, shame, and scandal. In his introduction, Mr. Lamont points out that some of the outstanding leaders of the A.C.L.U. who were especially active in removing Miss Flynn included John Haynes Holmes of New York's Community Church; Norman Thomas, the veteran Socialist leader and grand old man of the American Left; and Morris Ernst, who successfully maintained his double life of being co-counsel of the A.C.L.U. and personal attorney of J. Edgar Hoover. It was this celebrated liberal, Ernst, who led the group of "purgers" against Miss Flynn, and who, in his customary fashion, insisted upon calling her Elizabeth during the trial.

Behind this group of distinguished community leaders, who were covering their moral cowardice with such a show of virtue, alarm, and indignation, were of course the historical forces which induced their hypocrisy. Under the duress of the Nazi-Soviet pact in the early years of the Second World War, public opinion in the United States was inflamed against the leading civil liberties organization which, just a year before, in 1939, had proclaimed its intention of defending Communists among other victims of social injustice. Elizabeth Gurley Flynn, a founding member of the American Civil Liberties Union and twice elected to its Board, was a proclaimed, a most fiery, eloquent, and outstanding Communist. But in 1940 came the famous "Purge Resolution" which proclaimed that A.C.L.U. would not accept either Communists or Fascists in its official ranks—not that many Fascists had ever joined this organization, which indeed had, from its very inception, as Miss Flynn took pleasure in stating, included members of the IWW, revolutionary socialists, anarchists, and atheists in its leadership.

The 1940 Purge Resolution reversed the whole history of the A.C.L.U. and destroyed the struggle for American civil liberties at the very core of its existence. Meanwhile the indefatigable Morris Ernst (along with A.C.L.U.'s co-counsel Arthur Garfield Hays) was making a private deal with Congressman Martin Dies that if the recently established House Committee on Un-American Activities would only leave them alone, they would clean house themselves.

This was the classic American example of Instant Censorship on the Do-It-Yourself-Plan. In recent years I remember a very similar deal between Norman Cousins and his close friend, Senator Thomas Dodd of Connecticut—that ardent patriot—with respect to SANE, which in my own view has never recovered from its self-inflicted wounds.

Has the American Civil Liberties Union destroyed itself as a moral force in the history of American civil rights? (I am not discussing the various local branch chapters which have to a certain degree followed their own consciences and have done good work; the historical question is larger than that.) It is ironical that Mr. Lamont's book is published just after the A.C.L.U. made an attempt, in 1967–1968, to revise and repudiate the Purge Resolutions of an earlier period—an attempt, however, that ended up with a compromise, which, as Roger Baldwin told Corliss Lamont, was no compromise. "It's the same thing, but better expressed." The Old Guard triumphant has never paused to consider the cost of the triumph. Sanctimonious hypocrisy on their part has led to complete self-delusion; they do not even realize how they have betrayed their cultural heritage. Meanwhile, in *The Trial of Elizabeth Gurley Flynn*, we come directly to the illuminating and mysterious Transcript of their secret behavior, which is in itself such a drama, and a reflection in microcosm of similar convulsions in the national psyche during the Cold War trauma.

I regret I can only give you a taste of this. Dr. John

Haynes Holmes was the Board's chairman and, throwing all legal precedent aside according to his own whim, was also Chief Inquisitor presiding at Miss Flynn's pre-arranged demise. He is, to put it bluntly, horrid. But hardly less disgusting was the dramatist Elmer Rice, much to my surprise, who surrounded his vicious anti-Communism with lofty moral scruples. There is nothing in the world worse, as our own period has proved, than a liberal or formerly radical artist "atoning" for his guilt. (John Dos Passos has shown this; Arthur Miller promises to; and it is sad now to see that the James Wechsler of that period, then assistant editor of *The Nation*, was among those who defended Miss Flynn.) But Elmer Rice is voluble at this trial, and arrogant; while Morris Ernst, having developed the whole frame-up, is friendly— even palsy-walsy. Alas for the idols of our youth in all these cases; and meanwhile Norman Thomas was hardly less than vicious in his denunciations of the "Communist-dominated" American Civil Liberties Board.

The spirit of Dr. Harry F. Ward—to whom the book is dedicated—presides over the death-throes of the American Civil Liberties Union in 1940: an organization which, as he said when resigning, was not the same organization he had dedicated so much of his life to. The spirit of Roger Baldwin, although he was never a member of the Board, presided over, not really the legal lynching of Miss Flynn so much as the dissolution of a truly libertarian culture. There were heroes too on this Board (the final vote was a tie until Dr. Holmes broke it), and there are some oddly comic minor figures performing as small spirits always perform in moments of crisis.

To this central drama of the hidden transcript in *The Trial of Elizabeth Gurley Flynn*, Mr. Lamont has added the crucial historical documents of the trial and the period— documents alike of suppression and dissent. This book is an invaluable record, as I say, yet the end-effect is also rather curiously quaint—as though recalling some pleasanter and *nicer* period of social repression than we have faced since, or may have to face. This was only a *beginning*, this abdication of responsibility by the presiding Board of the American Civil Liberties Union in the face of a national hysteria. What was tragic then, and seems slightly comic today, might just end up as farce. It was Mark Twain who reminded us that, "It is by the goodness of God that in our country we have those three unspeakably precious things: freedom of speech, freedom of conscience, and the prudence never to practice either of them."

INTRODUCTION

One of the most unusual heresy trials on record is that of the late Elizabeth Gurley Flynn (1890–1964) by the Board of Directors of the American Civil Liberties Union on Tuesday night, May 7, 1940, at the City Club of New York, 55 West 44th Street. As a Director I was present at this extraordinary meeting which found, 10–9, Miss Flynn unfit to remain on the Board on the grounds that she was a member of the Communist Party, and on two minor charges. Although the trial took place more than twenty-eight years ago, I vividly recall the long and often acrimonious discussion that did not end until approximately 2:20 in the morning. Those six hours of tense debate constituted a great civil liberties drama.

This book reproduces the stenographic transcript of the proceedings made by the National Reporting Company of New York City. It also includes the most important exhibits that became part of the trial record, as well as other documents alluded to by Miss Flynn in her testimony. The complete transcript, heretofore virtually inaccessible to readers and researchers, is here published for the first time. Though the text of the Flynn trial is one of the most significant documents in the history of American civil liberties and the Civil Liberties Union, the national headquarters of that organization in New York City reports that it does not possess even one copy. Less than half of the transcript is to be found among the extensive papers deposited by the A.C.L.U. in the Rare Books and Special Collections section of the Princeton University Library.

During these many years, however, I have had an unabridged copy of the Flynn transcript in my files. I am at last making the document public because I consider it of great importance for the historical record; because it can teach present workers for civil liberties the disastrous consequences of compromising on their basic principles; and because it may serve as some stimulus to the Civil Liberties Union to eliminate permanently any and all provisos for political disclaimers on the part of its officers and staff. Members and officers of the A.C.L.U. need to be reminded of the witch-hunt that took place within their own organization.

When in 1633 the Catholic Inquisition in Rome brought Galileo to trial for his heretical views in astronomy, it was a crass violation of freedom of thought. But in those times there was no accepted tradition of free speech in the Western World. Nor was there any established rule, principle or procedure under which officials of the Catholic Church pledged themselves to uphold civil liberties. The terrible thing about the trial of Elizabeth Gurley Flynn is that it took place in this country almost 150 years after the Bill of Rights was adopted; and that it was carried through by the first and chief organization in the United States to have as its sole purpose the defense of civil liberties for all individuals and organizations, whatever their political or other views, within the U.S.A.

Furthermore, some of the outstanding leaders of the A.C.L.U. were especially active in the removal of Miss Flynn. These included John Haynes Holmes, Chairman of the Board of Directors and minister of the Community Church of New York City; Norman Thomas, veteran Socialist leader, well-known pacifist and a charter member of the Union; and Morris L. Ernst, co-counsel of the Civil Liberties Union and for many years personal attorney for J. Edgar Hoover of the Federal Bureau of Investigation. Mr. Ernst was the chief spokesman of the Board group seeking the ouster of Miss Flynn.

Roger N. Baldwin, Director of the Union from its founding in 1920 until 1950, was not a member of the Board of Directors and so had no vote at the Flynn trial. But he was pulling strings behind the scenes in all the maneuverings that led to the hearing. And it was he who persuaded Mrs. Dorothy Dunbar Bromley, woman's page columnist for the Scripps-Howard newspapers, to bring the charge against Elizabeth Flynn arising from her membership in the Communist Party. He chose Mrs. Bromley because he thought it would look better to have a woman initiate the proceedings against Miss Flynn. "It's a tough job," Baldwin wrote Mrs. Bromley, "but you are the person to do it with firmness and delicacy."*

As the Director of the A.C.L.U. Roger Baldwin exercised more initiative and wielded more power than any other individual connected with the organization. Had he chosen to uphold without compromise the basic principles of the Civil Liberties Union, the Flynn trial would never have taken place. His responsibility for this unhappy event was greater than that of anyone else.

I remember Elizabeth Flynn as a handsome woman, straightforward and hard-hitting in argument, whose face and voice gave the impression of great strength and sincerity of character. Mrs. Lucille Milner, Secretary of the A.C.L.U. for many years, describes her: "She was a warm, vital person, all Irish, with crystal blue eyes, a clear white skin and shining black hair which she parted in the middle and rolled back softly in a knot at the back. Her spirit and enthusiasm were contagious. I have not forgotten her famous pep talks at labor rallies when she stirred her audiences of working people to a high pitch." **

As for the trial itself, Mrs. Milner writes: "I looked at the accused. Elizabeth was now in her fifties, still beautiful; her

---

* Quoted by Lucille Milner, *Education of an American Liberal* (New York: Horizon Press, 1954), p. 282.
** *Ibid.*, p. 272.

blue eyes were calm, her manner self-possessed. . . . There was no question that Elizabeth was respected by everyone around the table, even by those who had instituted these proceedings, for her life-long concern for the oppressed and her passionate sense of justice. For a generation she had been a national figure in the liberal and labor movements; no one had ever challenged her devotion to civil liberties. . . ."*

Indeed, for more than three decades Elizabeth Flynn had been one of the staunchest fighters for the Bill of Rights in America. A charter member of the A.C.L.U., she not only fought for the free speech of others, but also battled for her own freedom of expression by speaking out on unpopular issues of the day. As one of the early I.W.W. (Industrial Workers of the World) leaders, she was repeatedly arrested while taking part in picket lines and demonstrations. Miss Flynn was one of the most active leaders in the big Paterson, N.J., strike of silk workers in 1913 and in the even bigger Passaic, N.J., strike of textile workers in 1926.**

Thus she made a telling point when she asked at the A.C.L.U. hearing: "Is there any member of this Board whose record as a consistent militant fighter for these rights can outweigh the records of William Z. Foster [labor leader and Communist Party official] and myself, since the first free speech fight in Spokane, Wash., in 1910, which was not our first arrests?"†

On March 4, 1940, the A.C.L.U. Board of Directors, at its regular meeting, passed a resolution offered by Mrs. Bromley, requesting Elizabeth Flynn to resign in view of the Board's decision to exclude Communists. When Miss Flynn declined to accede to this request, Mrs. Bromley read into the minutes the first and main charge against Miss Flynn, that "she is not

* *Ibid.*, pp. 276–77.
** For an account of Elizabeth Gurley Flynn's life through 1926, see her autobiography, *I Speak My Own Piece* (New York: Masses & Mainstream, 1955).
† See p. 105.

entitled to retain directorship on the Board on the ground that she is a member of the Communist Party."

The second charge, filed later by playwright Elmer Rice, was that Miss Flynn was disqualified from serving on the Board because she had made what he considered inappropriate remarks about members of the Board in an article in the March 19, 1940, issue of the *New Masses*,* a left-wing weekly.

The third charge, submitted by Roger William Riis, public relations counsel, was that Miss Flynn was unfit to remain on the Board by virtue of hostile comments she made about it in an article in the March 17, 1940, issue of the *Daily Worker*,** a Communist publication.

The second and third charges, both of which were sustained, were clearly subordinate to the first charge. Miss Flynn's two articles attacking the A.C.L.U. Board of Directors were obviously part of a broader and more fundamental controversy. They constituted Miss Flynn's first line of defense *after* the first charge had been filed against her. Intemperate as were some of her remarks, it is unlikely that the purge majority would have voted to throw out Miss Flynn on grounds of rudeness unless at the same time she happened to be a member of the Communist Party.

It is pertinent to note here that as far back as December 16, 1939, Mr. Norman Thomas had written an article for the *Call*,† official organ of the Socialist Party, in which he called for a purge of alleged Communists and fellow-travelers on the Board of the A.C.L.U. and accused such persons of hypocrisy. Although a special subcommittee reported to the Board that Thomas's article was "highly improper," the Board refused to take any action on the matter.

As I read the trial transcript again after many years, I once more feel shocked at the dishonesty and injustice of the pro-

* See p. 157.
** See p. 153.
† See p. 147.

ceedings, and at the extent to which they violate the fundamental tenets of civil liberties. One of the most important of all guarantees for civil libertarians is the stipulation in the Fifth Amendment that no person shall be "deprived of life, liberty, or property, without due process of law." Though the A.C.L.U. Board was not functioning as a court in the Flynn hearing, it had the obligation to act towards Miss Flynn in the spirit of "due process."

I believe that in the first place the Board disregarded due process in its haste to get rid of Miss Flynn in one session. The Chairman and others repeatedly noted the pressure of time. When the debate had gone on for more than three hours, Raymond Wise spoke up as follows: "I make another motion, Mr. Chairman. In the interests of a fair trial for Miss Flynn, I move we adjourn. This is a motion that doesn't have to be seconded, and doesn't have to be voted on, but I make it on this record. It is now twenty minutes to twelve." *

Obviously, Mr. Wise was correct in his estimate of the situation. After more than three hours of intense discussion requiring unflagging concentration of mind, everyone at the trial was tired. Some were groggy; it was difficult to think clearly. The hearing should have adjourned by midnight at the latest and then reconvened at a subsequent date. That would have been the proper procedure to ensure due process. Nobody supported Mr. Wise's motion, though I, for one, should have done so. When his motion failed, he withdrew from the meeting.

Early in her defense speech, Elizabeth Flynn raised the question of lack of due process. "I insist," she said, "that this Board has demonstrated its incapacity to serve as an impartial jury to hear any charges against me. Mrs. Bromley, Mr. Rice, Mr. Riis and Dr. Holmes cannot surely qualify since they have assumed the roles of complainants. It is inappropriate for those

* See p. 135.

who voted for the resolution* to act as my jury. Dr. Holmes is doubly disqualified by his statement that I am *a symbol of difficulties* and that my resignation—'requested and refused— would go far to resolve them. . . .' I demand the kind of trial the A.C.L.U. has insisted upon for the persons it defends."**

Dr. Holmes, sitting in the role of judge at the hearing, overruled each of these objections made by Miss Flynn, and was sustained by a narrow majority of the Board. He had pre-judged the heretic as guilty long before the trial took place. And I could not help reflecting on the history of religion and thinking that the Reverend Holmes was really acting out the part of Grand Inquisitor.

It was he, stepping definitely out of his supposed role as impartial presiding officer, who broke the 9–9 tie vote on the charge based on Miss Flynn's belonging to the Communist Party. His vote made the crucial decision 10–9 against her.† The chairman of a board or committee customarily does not vote unless there is a tie. Although Dr. Holmes had a legal right to cast the deciding vote, he was not required to do so.

After the final votes were taken on the charges against Elizabeth Flynn and for her expulsion, the Board of Directors was in such a hurry to be rid of the business that it did not bother to recall Miss Flynn and tell her of the verdict. In a let-ter to the Board on the next day, she protested vigorously against this final violation of due process. Her letter reads in part:

"At the conclusion of your deliberations, you adjourned the meeting and neither the Board nor the Chairman, or Mr. Baldwin, the Director, did me the common courtesy or ex-tended to me the legal right to call me back before the Board while in session and notify me of your decisions on my case.

* This refers to the A.C.L.U. Resolution of February 5, 1940. See p. 44.
** See pp. 49-50.
† See p. 176.

In fact, I was not notified by any officer of the Union afterwards either, in a formal manner. Even the meanest criminal in a court of law is allowed to receive the verdict of their [his] jury face to face. Yet I, who am a charter member of the American Civil Liberties Union, was denied this right by you. I learned some details of your decisions at the adjourned informal gathering of both majority and minority in the lounge room of the Hotel Algonquin next door, where at least hunger and thirst were unanimous! . . ." *

Item No. 4 in the Board Minutes of May 13, 1940, states: "Miss Flynn's letter taking exception to certain aspects of the May 7th hearing including the Board's failure to recall her after the vote of removal was taken, was read and filed together with Dr. Holmes's and Mr. Baldwin's letters of apology."

Miss Flynn's membership on the Board of Directors did not terminate at once. For under the by-laws of the Civil Liberties Union, expulsion from the Board had to be ratified by the National Committee composed of some fifty individuals scattered throughout the country. The A.C.L.U. office polled the members of this committee, and three months later the result was announced. Out of 51 members, a bare majority of 27 voted to uphold the Board's action; 12 opposed it, and the remaining 12 declined to vote.** Elizabeth Flynn's membership on the Board officially came to an end as of August 12, 1940.

On the same day the Board passed the following resolution and sent a copy to Miss Flynn: "The Board expressed its appreciation of Miss Flynn's long service to the cause of civil liberty and its regret at feeling obliged to act, in the light of changed circumstances, to terminate her association with the Union." At the same time Miss Flynn received letters express-

* *Daily Worker*, May 9, 1940.
** For the full record of the National Committee's vote, see Appendix Eight, p. 224.

ing sorrow and affection from Dr. Holmes and Mr. Baldwin. Speaking of them later, she said, "They sounded like this to me: 'So sorry. We must shoot you before breakfast. But we really love you. No hard feelings, we hope.' " *

In the entire six hours of debate at the trial no member of the Board, however bitterly opposed to Miss Flynn, could cite a single instance in which she had written, spoken or acted in violation of the Bill of Rights or the acknowledged principles of the Civil Liberties Union. Her expulsion on the first charge was grounded solely upon membership in a political group, the Communist Party, that had become the object of widespread hatred and fear throughout the United States. In short, the Board of Directors, instead of acting according to the criterion of *individual* guilt insisted upon repeatedly by the U.S. Supreme Court, again violated due process by judging Miss Flynn on the basis of "guilt by association."

This pernicious and unconstitutional principle the A.C.L.U. had constantly fought against in the past. But the organization had officially incorporated it in the purge Resolution of February 5, 1940. That resolution of course played a central role in the Flynn trial and reads in part: **

"The Board of Directors and the National Committee of the American Civil Liberties Union . . . hold it inappropriate for any person to serve on the governing committees of the Union or on its staff, who is a member of any political organization which supports totalitarian dictatorship in any country, or who by his public declarations indicates his support of such a principle.

"Within this category we include organizations in the United States supporting the totalitarian governments of the Soviet Union and of the Fascist and Nazi countries (such as the

* Elizabeth Gurley Flynn, "The A.C.L.U. Regrets To Kick Me Out," *Sunday Worker*, Sept. 22, 1940.
** For full text of the resolution, see p. 44.

Communist Party, the German-American Bund and others); as well as native organizations with obvious anti-democratic objectives or practices."

Since the above resolution was vital to the case against Elizabeth Flynn under the first charge, she naturally wanted to deal with it in some detail in defending herself. Hence the first half of the trial was devoted in large measure to the question of whether there should be introduced into the record certain letters opposing the 1940 Resolution written to the A.C.L.U. by some of its officers and several affiliates. The Board of Directors finally voted that all such material should be excluded as "irrelevant." They thereby seriously handicapped Miss Flynn's defense and transgressed once more the equitable procedure known as due process.

The 1940 Resolution was directly contrary to the traditional policy of the Civil Liberties Union. The Board of Directors had reaffirmed that policy in an official leaflet issued in April, 1939, entitled *Why We Defend Free Speech for Nazis, Fascists and Communists*.* This brochure declared: "The Union does not engage in political controversy. It takes no position on any political or economic issue or system. It defends without favoritism the rights of all-comers, whatever their political or economic views. It is wholly unconcerned with movements abroad or with foreign governments."

Why did the A.C.L.U. Board change its mind between April, 1939, and February, 1940? There were two main reasons. First, the Nazi-Soviet non-aggression pact in August, 1939, the outbreak of World War II in September and the Soviet invasion of Finland in November led to increasing tensions among Americans, and to renewed hostility towards the Soviet Union and Communists in general. These various factors combined to create an influential group within the Board of the A.C.L.U. which was more interested in fighting *against*

---

* For full text, see Appendix One, p. 183.

22

Communists than *for* civil liberties and which also viewed the purge resolution as a strategic measure for the appeasement of the strong anti-Communist elements in the community.

Second, the two general counsel of the A.C.L.U., Morris Ernst and Arthur Garfield Hays, had a cocktail conference in October, 1939, with Representative Martin Dies, Chairman of the recently established House Committee on Un-American Activities, at the Hay-Adams House in Washington, D.C. After this conference, Representative Dies and his Committee stopped claiming that the Civil Liberties Union was a Communist front. And Mr. Dies suddenly gave the A.C.L.U. a clean bill of health by declaring that "there was not any evidence that the American Civil Liberties Union was a Communist organization."

There is abundant circumstantial evidence to show that Martin Dies suddenly switched policy towards the A.C.L.U. because he was assured at the off-the-record Washington conference that the organization itself would take the necessary steps to "cleanse" itself of Communists. These steps, of course, it put into effect with the 1940 Resolution and the Flynn expulsion.

The first indication of a deal with Dies came earlier when, during December, 1939, the purge group on the Board of Directors tried unsuccessfully to put through a weak and vacillating report on the Un-American Activities Committee. Speaking later of this report, Mr. Osmond Fraenkel, always one of the most uncompromising Directors, stated that "it would have been a shocking disgrace to the Union had that original report been allowed to stand unchanged. It was an unworthy attempt to curry favor with Mr. Dies."*

In a special press release explaining the 1940 Resolution, Mr. Baldwin as Director of the A.C.L.U. acknowledged the

---

* Letter to John Haynes Holmes of Sept. 5, 1940. Now in the Archives of the American Civil Liberties Union at the Princeton University Library.

impact of foreign affairs on the Board's action. The release said in part: "The occasion for raising this issue at this time is the increasing tension which has resulted everywhere from the direction of the Communist international movement since the Soviet-Nazi pact. The abandonment of the struggle against Fascism and the other changes in Communist policy have raised sharp issues which were reflected in the attitude of members of our Board of Directors." *

In the same release Mr. Baldwin, hard-pressed to show consistency in the A.C.L.U.'s action, made the false assertion that "The present resolution merely states what has been always the unwritten policy of the Union in elections or appointments." The truth is that Anna Rochester had been elected to the Board of Directors and William Z. Foster to the National Committee when it was well known that they belonged to the Communist Party. Also Miss Flynn was unanimously re-elected to the Board in 1939 two years after she had openly stated at a Board meeting that she had joined the Communist Party. When she made this announcement, neither Baldwin nor any member of the Board made any objection.**

The Resolution of 1940, a thinly disguised Loyalty Oath, and the Flynn expulsion following from it, constituted a gross betrayal of the Bill of Rights by the American Civil Liberties Union. The evil effects were immediate and far-reaching. The resolution, the first of its kind to be adopted by a liberal organization in the United States, became a precedent and a model for all sorts of other organizations and for government agencies. Trade unions, youth groups and civic organizations throughout the country passed similar resolutions. One result in the Civil Liberties Union itself was that its National Office checked with J. Edgar Hoover as to whether one individual or another was a member of the Communist Party.

* For the full text, see Appendix Two, p. 187.
** See p. 99.

24

It became ludicrous for the A.C.L.U. to object to government political purges, as when in the summer of 1940 it protested the firing in New York City of some 1,000 W.P.A. (Works Projects Administration) workers alleged to be "subversives." On June 25, 1940, the Union attacked this purge as a "deprivation of civil rights wholly without justification" and stated that the dismissal of Communists and Bund members "was indefensible so long as they belonged to legal organizations functioning openly."

The A.C.L.U. Resolution of 1940 meant a major setback for civil liberties in America and helped sow the seeds for the U.S. witch-hunt that followed World War II. That witch-hunt, culminating in the nation-wide movement known as McCarthyism, revolved around the alleged Communist menace and constantly utilized the doctrine of "guilt by association" as one of its main weapons.

Although the resolution received a great deal of favorable newspaper publicity, it raised a storm of protest among civil libertarians in general and among members, officers and affiliates of the A.C.L.U. Many affiliates expressed complete opposition. One of the most effective protests came from a group of seventeen prominent liberals who wrote an Open Letter to the Civil Liberties Union.* They asserted in part:

"We appeal to the American Civil Liberties Union to rescind its recent purge resolution as unworthy of its traditions and incompatible with its principles. . . . We believe that by the purge resolution the American Civil Liberties Union encourages the very tendencies it was intended to fight. It sets an example less liberal organizations will not be slow to follow. . . . The phrasing of the purge resolution is so wide as to make the Civil Liberties Union seem a fellow-traveler of the Dies Committee. Its context is such as to make it seem that the Civil

* For full text and signatories, see Appendix Three, p. 189.

Liberties Union has been unable to keep its head in the kind of crisis that is the greatest danger to civil liberties."

Roger Baldwin himself had given a convincing criticism of the idea behind the 1940 Resolution, *before it was passed*, when he wrote novelist John Dos Passos on December 4, 1939: "I don't believe that however any of us feel about Communists, we can afford to take the position of excluding anybody from the Union because of political views, or to remove from our Board anybody whose views of international affairs differ from the majority. Once we begin drawing such a line, there is no end to it. . . ." * This letter was in answer to one from Dos Passos resigning from the National Committee of the A.C.L.U. because the organization had not up till that time adopted an anti-Communist position.

In 1951 the A.C.L.U. Board of Directors gave added standing and permanency to the 1940 Resolution by incorporating it into the organization's Constitution, which can only be amended by a two-thirds majority of the A.C.L.U. electors. However, the skeleton in the closet of the Civil Liberties Union has kept rattling loudly. A broad movement for repeal of the resolution, initiated by the more militant affiliates of the Union, won official recognition in January of 1966 when the Board of Directors appointed a Special Committee to study the 1940 Resolution.

During discussion on the recommendations of this committee, the Union took a forward step in March, 1967, when it decided to drop from the organization's membership card the following statement of long standing: "The A.C.L.U. needs and welcomes the support of all those—and only those—whose devotion to civil liberties is not qualified by adherence to Communist, Fascist, K.K.K. or other totalitarian doctrine."

At the same time the A.C.L.U. placed in its Constitution

* Now in the Archives of the American Civil Liberties Union at the Princeton University Library.

an Objects Clause, Section 2, that was recommended by the Special Committee. It reads: "The object of the American Civil Liberties Union shall be to maintain and advance civil liberties, including the freedom of association, press, religion and speech, and the rights to the franchise, to due process of law, and to equal protection of the laws for all people throughout the United States and its possessions. The Union's objects shall be sought wholly without political partisanship."

The Special Committee further recommended that the 1940 Resolution be supplanted by the simple statement that officers and staff members of the A.C.L.U. be "unequivocally committed to the objectives of this Union" as set forth in the Objects Clause.

After a long debate this sensible formulation was rejected by the Civil Liberties Union. Instead it voted into effect two new provisions as a "compromise" to supersede the 1940 Resolution. The first, adopted in April 1968 as Section 7 (D) of the Constitution, reads: "All persons who are members of the national Board of Directors, the National Committee or the board of an affiliate (or chapter), or a committee or other agency of any of the above, and all persons who are members of any staff, shall be unequivocally committed to the objects of this Union as set forth in Section 2 above, and *to the concept of democratic government and civil liberties for all people*." [Italics mine.—C.L.]

The words "all people" in the phrase I have italicized presumably mean all people throughout the world. The language of the Objects Clause, "all people throughout the United States and its possessions" is carefully omitted. Hence Section 7 (D) automatically brings the Civil Liberties Union back to the 1940 Resolution and enables it, for instance, to bar as officers those who give moral support to some foreign state, perhaps one recently freed from colonialism, that considers certain non-democratic controls justified.

27

The second and more objectionable provision, adopted by the Board of Directors as the official "interpretation" of the statement I have just discussed, reads:

"Whereas long-established policy has made clear that the leadership of the Union should be devoted unequivocally to the principles of civil liberties; and

"Whereas, a current statement of that policy is desirable as an interpretation of the constitutional requirement for unequivocal commitment to those principles;

"Therefore, be it resolved that the interpretation of the requirement stated in Section 7 (D) should be understood to preclude support of those principles which reject or qualify individual liberties and minority rights for all people equally, regardless of race, sex, religion or opinion; *or which reject or qualify the freedoms associated with the forms and processes of political democracy.* [Italics mine.—C.L.]

"It is further resolved that in the event of any question arising as to the application of this policy, it shall be dealt with by the appropriate responsible board, and in disputed cases arising in affiliates by the National Board on appeal."

In the third paragraph of the above statement the phrase "all people" again is reminiscent of the 1940 Resolution, because it involves the Civil Liberties Union in determining which foreign governments "reject or qualify minority rights" and what individuals are then to be excluded.

The clause that I have italicized is so broad and vague that it could apply to most political scientists and commentators on public affairs. It could be used, for instance, against Americans who think that the "processes of political democracy" in the United States are insufficient and who therefore resort to civil disobedience on behalf of international peace or civil rights for the Negro people. As applied to foreign countries, this clause could be turned against those who are sympathetic in general to some foreign democracy which, like France under President de Gaulle, sees fit to *qualify* certain freedoms.

The wording of the clause invites another Flynn-type trial whenever pressures for conformity mount, as in the McCarthy period, or whenever some officer of the A.C.L.U. or of an affiliate comes to disagree with the Union's official line on democracy. The italicized passage is open to so many varying definitions that it resembles that part of the resolution establishing the House Committee on Un-American Activities which gives it the power to investigate those who "attack the principle of the form of government as guaranteed by our Constitution." The Civil Liberties Union itself pointed out that this language is "dangerously vague" and that imprecision in a governmental statute makes it unconstitutional because no individual knows when he is or is not violating the law.

The last paragraph of the second A.C.L.U. statement is ominous, because it goes beyond the 1940 Resolution to establish a definite procedure on how to deal with civil liberties heretics who are not deemed fit to serve on the governing bodies or staff of the A.C.L.U. Also this section makes doubly clear that all affiliates and chapters of the organization must carry out the exclusion policies, whereas several affiliates refused to accept the 1940 Resolution.

In my judgment the new and complex statements setting up qualifications for A.C.L.U. officers and staff members add up to a political disclaimer or loyalty test that has little more merit than the 1940 Resolution. This interpretation is supported by what Roger Baldwin, who helped draft the 1968 Resolutions, said to me when I told him I had heard a "compromise" went through at the Civil Liberties Union in place of the 1940 Resolution. "It was no compromise," he replied. "It's the same thing, but better expressed."

The principles of political purity enunciated in the 1968 Resolutions must be accepted by every person who becomes an officer or staff member of the Civil Liberties Union or an affiliate. If any person nominated for office or suggested for the staff is challenged as not believing in the new civil liberties orthodoxy proclaimed in these statements, he must show that he supports them or be rejected as a candidate. In doubtful cases the National Board of the A.C.L.U., acting as a sort of subversive thoughts control agency, will make the final decision.

While the Civil Liberties Union does much useful work, it can never function with a clear conscience and win the unqualified support of principled civil libertarians until it rescinds its new "loyalty" resolutions and repudiates the action of the 1940 Board of Directors in expelling Miss Flynn. During the past decade the U.S. courts have increasingly ruled out government Loyalty Oaths as violative of the First Amendment. The A.C.L.U. in its internal functioning has the obligation to be at least as faithful to the Bill of Rights as our courts.

But I have said enough. For all Americans who support the Bill of Rights, for all members and officers of civil liberties organizations, for all those who believe in the principles of democracy, the record of the trial of Elizabeth Gurley Flynn speaks for itself and will continue to speak in the on-going struggle for freedom.

Corliss Lamont

New York City
June 1968

Members of the Board of Directors of the American Civil Liberties Union Present at Trial of Elizabeth Gurley Flynn, May 7, 1940

Alfred M. Bingham, writer and editor of a liberal journal, *Common Sense*

Mrs. Dorothy Dunbar Bromley, columnist for Scripps-Howard newspapers

Carl Carmer, author

Robert W. Dunn, Executive Secretary, Labor Research Association

Morris L. Ernst, lawyer and co-counsel of A.C.L.U.

John F. Finerty, lawyer

Miss Elizabeth Gurley Flynn, member of National Committee of the Communist Party, U.S.A.

Osmond K. Fraenkel, lawyer

Walter Frank, lawyer

Nathan Greene, lawyer

Arthur Garfield Hays, lawyer and co-counsel of A.C.L.U.

Rev. John Haynes Holmes, Chairman, Board of Directors, A.C.L.U., and presiding officer at trial

Ben W. Huebsch, publisher and treasurer of A.C.L.U.

Abraham J. Isserman, lawyer

Miss Dorothy Kenyon, lawyer

Dr. Corliss Lamont, author and teacher

Miss Florina Lasker, philanthropist
William L. Nunn, teacher
Elmer Rice, author and playwright
Roger W. Riis, writer and publicist
Whitney North Seymour, lawyer
Rev. William B. Spofford, Protestant Episcopal Church
Raymond L. Wise, lawyer

Non-Voting Members of A.C.L.U. Staff Present

Roger N. Baldwin, Director
Lucille B. Milner, Secretary

Members of the Board Not Present at Trial

Harry Binsse, writer and editor
John Chamberlain, writer and editor
Richard S. Childs, organization executive and publicist
Lester B. Granger, Executive Director, Urban League
Quincy Howe, writer and editor
Thurgood Marshall, lawyer (now a Justice of the United
    States Supreme Court)
Eliot Pratt, philanthropist
Norman Thomas, Socialist leader and pacifist
Mary Van Kleeck, industrial sociologist

PART I

TRANSCRIPT OF THE TRIAL

A meeting of the Board of Directors of the American Civil Liberties Union was held at eight o'clock on Tuesday evening, May 7, 1940, at the City Club of New York, 55 West 44th Street, New York City, Dr. John Haynes Holmes presiding.

Chairman Holmes: Will the meeting please come to order? I was waiting for Mr. Riis, but I judge he will be here in a moment.

On the fifth day of February, 1940, this Board of Directors passed a certain resolution which is familiar to you all, and which has been widely discussed publicly. This resolution, I think, I need not read; it will be entered on the minutes at the proper place.

On March 4, 1940, on the basis of the resolution, Mrs. Dorothy Dunbar Bromley submitted to this Board charges addressed to Elizabeth Gurley Flynn, a member of our Board of Directors.

Following these charges, an article written by Miss Flynn appeared in the *Daily Worker* under date of March 17; and, on March 19, another article written by Miss Flynn was published in the *New Masses*. On the basis of the *New Masses* article of March 19, Elmer Rice, on March 25, submitted an additional charge against Miss Flynn. On April 8, Mr. Roger William Riis submitted still another charge, based on the *Daily Worker* article of March 17. That makes three charges in all.

We have met here tonight for the consideration of these charges and to give to Miss Flynn the hearing to which she is properly entitled. The office of the American Civil Liberties Union has drawn up a suggested order of business for our consideration and, I trust, our acceptance. Copies of this order of business are before you.

It provides for a reading of the by-laws, the minutes of the meetings at which the charges were filed, and the notices sent to Miss Flynn by Mrs. Milner. Secondly, it provides for a presentation of evidence on the first charge by Mrs. Bromley; then a presentation of evidence on the second charge by Mr. Riis; and then a presentation of evidence on the third charge by Mr. Rice.

The next order of business will be Miss Flynn's reply to these charges in due order. This is to be followed by a discussion, first, of the charges, and then of the action, if any, to be taken by this Board. Then there will be such votes—by ballot, it is suggested—as may be proper and may be desired.

Lastly, there will be a discussion of the statement to be issued by the office to the members of the Civil Liberties Union and to the press. In connection with this particular item, I am asked to request that no member of this Board give any statement to the representative of any newspaper. If inquiry is made by any reporter, I request that the reporter be referred to the office. The release should properly come from the office. It probably will be prepared here tonight, to be handled in due course by the office.

I should like to ask whether there is any objection to our proceeding tonight upon the basis of this order of business, as I have just read it. (Pause) If there is no objection, we will consider this the order of business of the evening.

Before proceeding, I might announce that we have a stenographer here who will take verbatim notes of everything that is said. I think it might be well if every person speaking be very careful to speak clearly, and I think I might suggest that it would be well if we have as little interruption and confusion as possible in the proceedings of this meeting, in order that we may have a good and a complete record.

I will ask from Mrs. Milner a reading of the by-laws of the Union governing our procedure tonight.

Mrs. Milner (Reading): "Any member of the Board of Directors may, after hearing and due cause shown, be expelled or suspended by majority vote of the other directors, subject to the approval of the active members, to be had in the same manner as for the election of directors."

Chairman Holmes: That covers that item?

Mrs. Milner: Yes.

Mr. Lamont: Mr. Chairman, as I understand it, that means that any decision here on expulsion has to be submitted to the National Committee for approval?

Mr. Baldwin: That's correct, yes.

Chairman Holmes: I will ask for a reading of the minutes of the meetings at which these charges were filed.

Mrs. Milner: You don't want the whole minutes, do you? You mean just the charges?

Chairman Holmes: Yes.

(Mrs. Milner read Item 13 of the Minutes of the meeting of the Board of Directors held March 4, 1940; Item 8 of the Minutes of the meeting held March 25, 1940; and Item 1 of the Minutes of the meeting held April 8, 1940.)

[Item 13 of the March 4th Minutes reads: "On motion of Mrs. Bromley, the following charge was ordered placed on the minutes: 'I hereby formulate the following charge against Elizabeth Gurley Flynn and ask that a hearing be held as to whether or not Miss Flynn be expelled on the basis of the charge that Elizabeth Gurley Flynn is not entitled to retain directorship on the Board on the ground that she is a member of the Communist Party.' "

[Item 8 of the March 25th Minutes reads: "Mr. Rice preferred and filed in writing the following charge: 'I hereby charge that Miss Flynn's article in the *New Masses* of March 19, 1940, disqualifies her from continued membership on the Board of the American Civil Liberties Union.' "

[Item 1 of the April 8th Minutes reads: "Mr. Riis preferred and filed in writing the following charge: 'I hereby charge that Miss Elizabeth Gurley Flynn's article in the *Daily Worker** of March 17, 1940, disqualifies her from continued membership on the Board of Directors of the American Civil Liberties Union.' "]

Chairman Holmes: I will ask you to read the notices sent to Miss Flynn covering these charges.

(Mrs. Milner read the notices referred to.)

Mr. Finerty: Mr. Chairman, in view of the fact that there has been no objection to the proceedings, I don't want to suggest any change; but I do think that Miss Flynn should be given the opportunity, if she desires, to have the evidence on each charge presented separately, and her answer made separately to each charge. I see no necessity for it, but I think it would be well to offer her that.

Chairman Holmes: Were you here when we adopted that order of business?

Mr. Finerty: I was.

Chairman Holmes: You want to offer that for reconsideration?

Mr. Finerty: I just make it as a suggestion to whoever is acting as counsel for Miss Flynn. I suggest that she be offered that opportunity.

Chairman Holmes: As I understand it, Miss Flynn, you are not availing yourself of the privilege of counsel?

Miss Flynn: No, I am not. I originally had asked Mr. Fraenkel to represent me as counsel, but, because I have not been able to confer with him and to consult with him on my procedure, I released him from that obligation. I presume that the lawyers who are here—members of the Board—will protect any legal rights that I have in the matter.

Chairman Holmes: Or Mr. Fraenkel himself, sitting informally at your right.

* The correct name for the publication here cited is *Sunday Worker.*
—Ed.

38

Mr. Finerty: On that ground then, particularly, I think it should be called to Miss Flynn's attention that she should have that privilege, if she so desires, of having evidence on the charges presented separately, and her replies made separately, and a separate vote on each charge.

Chairman Holmes: I heard no objection from Miss Flynn when we adopted the order, but I should like to ask now if it would be more satisfactory to you, Miss Flynn, if we presented the first charge and then heard your reply, and then the second charge—

Miss Flynn: And then took a vote on that?

Chairman Holmes: That would be a drastic change.

Mr. Frank: We want to keep this rather simple, I suppose. You don't mean by that that each charge will be considered separately in the sense that whatever may be said in relation to one charge will not be deemed equally said in relation to the other charges? Otherwise, you would have to repeat everything—if they are treated too separately.

Mr. Finerty: I do not think that is a practical procedure, but I think Miss Flynn should be given the opportunity of availing herself of that procedure if she sees fit.

Chairman Holmes: Do you desire to suggest any change to your own advantage, Miss Flynn?

Miss Flynn: Suppose I just state my conception of what the procedure was to be? I prepared a statement and in the statement I defended myself primarily against the first charge, on the assumption that if I were found guilty of the first charge and expelled from the Union, the other charges would no longer be important—reserving the right to defend myself subsequently on the other charges if there is a favorable decision on the first charge.

I wrote my statement myself, and it may not be perfect from a legal standpoint, but I have tried to embody in it my objections to procedure as well as my defense, so that it may be that I will have to divide it in two and read half at one time and half at another, or read it all together, as you prefer.

Chairman Holmes: I am sure we all desire to meet Miss Flynn's—

Miss Flynn: I am reserving my right to make objections to procedure, which I have embodied in the statement, because I don't know how to make all these motions that lawyers are so adept at making.

Chairman Holmes: We all desire, in so far as possible, to meet Miss Flynn's own desire and to carry on a procedure in accordance with her own preparation. I should be glad, therefore, to hear any motion, if anybody desires to make a motion, for changing this order of business. Otherwise, in the absence of any objection, I shall follow the order as we adopted it a moment ago.

Mr. Fraenkel: I will move, then, that the procedure as outlined be modified so that Miss Flynn be heard in answer to the first charge, and a vote taken on that, before we proceed to anything else.

Mr. Finerty: I second that.

Mr. Isserman: I should like to amend the motion, if I may, by adding a clause as follows: That any matter which Miss Flynn has by way of objection to procedure or the form of the charges or their sufficiency should be heard before there is presentation of any evidence.

I make that suggestion because Miss Flynn herself indicates that she has that type of objection prepared, and customarily that is the thing that is heard first.

Chairman Holmes: Objection to the whole procedure? Do I understand—

Mr. Isserman: Yes; if she has objections to the charges which are by way of going to their sufficiency or to the procedure as not being proper, it seems we should hear that before we give the evidence.

Chairman Holmes: If the Chair may rule, I think that

would not be necessary as an amendment, because it would be deemed proper that she should include in her answer to the first charge any statement to that effect. Would that be satisfactory?

Mr. Isserman: Not quite, because I suggest that, if she has that preliminary kind of motion, that should be heard before we present the evidence on the first charge.

Mr. Fraenkel: I accept that.

Chairman Holmes: And you, Mr. Finerty?

Mr. Finerty: Yes, I accept it.

Chairman Holmes: Are you ready for the question, or is there discussion? (Pause) If there is no discussion, we will vote upon the motion as amended. I think it is clear without restatement.

(The motion was put to a vote and carried.)

Chairman Holmes: In accordance with this resolution, I will ask Miss Flynn if she has any objection to the method of procedure which we are following tonight in accordance with our by-laws.

Mr. Fraenkel: In regard to the first charge?

Chairman Holmes: On the basis of the first charge. We are speaking now to the first charge, as I understand it.

Miss Flynn: You mean you want me to read that part of the statement in which I do protest against procedure?

Chairman Holmes: Against procedure itself—or would it be as satisfactory for you to do that after Mrs. Bromley has stated her charge?

Miss Flynn: Yes, it is satisfactory to me, so long as I do it.

Mr. Rice: I want to ask if Mrs. Milner had finished reading all the notices.

Mrs. Milner: Yes.

Chairman Holmes: If there is no objection, then we will hear from Mrs. Bromley, presenting the first charge.

41

Mr. Hays: May I ask first that our by-laws be read again?

(The by-laws of the Union governing the procedure of the meeting were read again.)

Mr. Finerty: May I inquire as to the definition of "active member"? Does that mean an active member of the Board of Directors or the National Committee?

Mr. Baldwin: The National Committee.

Mr. Isserman: On behalf of Miss Flynn—and she has appealed to the lawyers present—I believe it should be noted that the presentation of evidence without objection will not preclude her from making her motions to the validity of the whole procedure later.

Chairman Holmes: Very good.

Mr. Frank: Might I suggest to Mr. Isserman that this is not, of course, a trial in a law court? It is an informal hearing. We are supposed to discuss and argue and present what we wish without any formal rules whatsoever, and I don't think that anything that Miss Flynn may do during the course of the evening will in any way preclude her from doing something else later in the evening if she so sees fit. There are no technical preclusions in a hearing of this kind.

Mr. Isserman: I am glad that is noted on the record.

Mr. Hays: May I ask if it is held that none of the charges are due cause?

Miss Flynn: Certainly that would be my position.

Chairman Holmes: If there is no objection, we will ask Mrs. Bromley to present her evidence on the first charge. Then Miss Flynn will have the opportunity to reply, both as regards the procedure itself and the evidence presented on this first charge.

Mrs. Bromley: Mr. Chairman, I should like to offer in evidence a certified copy of the Resolution of February 5, 1940, with which the members of the Board are familiar. I will pass it down to Miss Flynn.

(The document referred to was handed to Miss Flynn.)

Mr. Fraenkel: Mr. Chairman, I thought that the position taken by Counsel was that this Resolution of February 5 was wholly irrelevant to the presentation of any charges. We are all familiar with the resolution and don't need a certified copy of it. I think it has no place in this proceeding.

Chairman Holmes: If there is no objection, the Chair will accept the resolution and ask that it be placed on the minutes.

Mr. Fraenkel: There is objection.

Chairman Holmes: You appeal from the ruling of the Chair, Mr. Fraenkel?

Mr. Fraenkel: If you overrule my objection, I appeal; yes.

Chairman Holmes: I shall have to rule that the resolution is relevant and should properly be entered upon the minutes. Mr. Fraenkel, as I understand, appeals from that ruling. That calls for a vote, does it not?

Mr. Lamont: Mr. Chairman, I believe that our Counsel, Mr. Hays, contradicted you some weeks ago when we discussed this. I should like to get his opinion on it again.

Mr. Hays: I say that under the by-laws we can expel a member of the Board of Directors for due cause and that the by-laws haven't been changed by that resolution. I think the resolution, however, might be some evidence in connection with what might be regarded as due cause, while they don't [it doesn't] amend the by-laws. I don't think it is conclusive by any means, but I think it is evidence on the subject.

Mr. Huebsch: This procedure doesn't seem to be in line with the method that Mr. Frank outlined a few minutes ago for the hearing. I don't see that it makes much difference, according to my lay mind, whether that is in or out; and if Mr. Fraenkel is going to make that kind of objection at the start, we are due here for one of those Senatorial sessions that require you to put the clock back every day.

Mr. Fraenkel: If it is understood that the acceptance of the resolution means nothing, I will withdraw my objection.

Chairman Holmes: Should I understand that your objection is withdrawn?

Mr. Finerty: I call for a vote on the appeal from the Chair.

Chairman Holmes: Do I understand the objection is withdrawn?

Mr. Fraenkel: No.

Mr. Finerty: I think the matter is relevant, though not conclusive. I call for a vote.

Chairman Holmes: Is there any further discussion? (Pause) If not, we will vote on a motion to support the Chair.

(The motion was put to a vote and carried.)

Chairman Holmes: The objection is overruled and the ruling of the Chair stands.

Mr. Isserman: I think some sort of mark should be put on this.

Mrs. Bromley: I will present it to the stenographer.

(The copy of the Resolution of February 5, 1940, was received in evidence and marked Exhibit No. 1.)

EXHIBIT NO. 1

A.C.L.U. Resolution of February 5, 1940

While the American Civil Liberties Union does not make any test of opinion on political or economic questions a condition of membership, and makes no distinction in defending the right to hold and utter any opinions, the personnel of its governing committees and staff is properly subject to the test of consistency in the defense of civil liberties in all aspects and all places.

That consistency is inevitably compromised by persons

who champion civil liberties in the United States and yet who justify or tolerate the denial of civil liberties by dictatorships abroad. Such a dual position in these days, when issues are far sharper and more profound, makes it desirable that the Civil Liberties Union make its position unmistakably clear.

The Board of Directors and the National Committee of the American Civil Liberties Union therefore hold it inappropriate for any person to serve on the governing committees of the Union or on its staff, who is a member of any political organization which supports totalitarian dictatorship in any country, or who by his public declarations indicates his support of such a principle.

Within this category we include organizations in the United States supporting the totalitarian governments of the Soviet Union and of the Fascist and Nazi countries (such as the Communist Party, the German-American Bund and others); as well as native organizations with obvious anti-democratic objectives or practices.

•

Chairman Holmes: Mrs. Bromley now has the floor, and I think it will be helpful to us all if she be permitted to make her statement without interruption.

Mrs. Bromley: I will speak very briefly, presenting my remarks in the form of two questions to Miss Flynn.

Does Miss Flynn concede that she is a member in good standing of the Communist Party as of now?

Miss Flynn: I presume I answer that in my statement.

Chairman Holmes: Do you desire an answer now, Mrs. Bromley?

Mrs. Bromley: Yes.

Miss Flynn: I don't concede that I have to answer, but of course I have no objection to answering that I am a member of the Communist Party in good standing.

Mrs. Bromley: That is the first question. The second is

just as simple: Do you concede that you are a member of good standing of the National Committee of the Communist Party?

Miss Flynn: Yes, certainly.

Mrs. Bromley: That is a policy-making committee, is it not?

Miss Flynn: Certainly—a policy-making committee between conventions.

Mrs. Bromley: Yes. That is all that I have to present in conjunction with the Resolution of February 5.

Chairman Holmes: Thank you, Miss Flynn. We should be glad to hear your reply.

Miss Flynn: It is a rather lengthy reply to two such brief questions, but it seems inevitable.

I want to say first that I appreciate the delay which was granted to me by the Board in these hearings.* I am sure that I might have made a better job of my defense if I had had a different period in which to prepare it, so I will ask the lawyers not to be too critical of it from a legal standpoint. I have mimeographed copies of my reply, which I will be very glad to distribute.

(Mimeographed copies of Miss Flynn's reply to Mrs. Bromley's charges were distributed to members of the Board. Miss Flynn then began to read the reply:)

ELIZABETH GURLEY FLYNN'S DEFENSE

This charge is based on the claim that I am not entitled to retain directorship on the Board of the American Civil Liberties Union because I am a member of the Communist Party of the U.S.A., under a resolution passed by the National Committee and Board of Directors on February 5th, 1940. (Copy of resolution to be made part of the record.)

* The trial was postponed from March 25 to May 7 owing to the illness and death of Miss Flynn's son, Fred Flynn.—Ed.

46

I challenge the validity of this entire procedure, but I answer the charge by stating categorically that I am a member of the Communist Party and no proof is necessary on this point. I move a dismissal of the charge on the ground that I am fully entitled to retain my directorship, that I cannot and should not be expelled because of membership in the Communist Party, that this proceeding is neither appropriate nor fair, since the resolution under which it is brought is contrary to the principles and purposes of the A.C.L.U. and violates its traditional policies as is clearly set forth in the resignation of Dr. Harry F. Ward, which I request be here made a part of my defense.

A resolution of "inappropriateness" is neither legal nor binding. In his reply to Messrs. Parsons, Meiklejohn and West, when they asked for reconsideration and reversal of this resolution as "false to the principles of the Union" and insisted upon a return to the traditional procedure of the Union, Dr. Holmes stated that "as long as it remains *a declaration of propriety*, one need not be too critical of the precise language used." The requests of these three members of our National Committee, as well as Prof. Lovett, Mrs. Gartz and others; of numerous active local committees, of individual members, of friends and sympathizers, for a reconsideration have thus far been ignored by this Board. I insist therefore, that all letters, resolutions, protests of members of the National Committee, members of the Board of Directors, active members and contributors to the A.C.L.U. be made an open part of this trial record. They demonstrate that this resolution does not meet with their unqualified approval; that it is a reversal and complete change of policy; that it is the subject of severe criticism, and is not considered constitutional or binding by our members. (All letters, telegrams, etc. received in office re Resolution, Dr. Ward's resignation, charges against Miss Flynn are to be considered part of record.)

I request further that there be included in this trial record certain publications of the A.C.L.U. to demonstrate such a *change of policy:* 1) "The A.C.L.U., Inc." of September 1938, from which I quote: "The National Committee and the Board of Directors represent every shade of economic and political opinion" and which listed as on our governing committees one Communist and three members "who express political or economic preference for the C.P."; and 2) the leaflet *Why We Defend Free Speech for Nazis, Fascists and Communists,** April, 1939, which declares, *"The Union does not engage in political controversy. It takes no position on any political or economic issue or system. . . . It is wholly unconcerned with movements abroad or with foreign governments."* These two published statements show clearly that the resolution conflicts with the basic positions of the Union, and is not, as Mr. Baldwin has repeatedly stated, "a slight extension of policy." I request the inclusion of the two issues of the leaflet, "Civil Liberties—Chief Issues" of June, 1939, in which no censorship over the views of its members is guaranteed, and of January, 1940, which is modified by the inclusion of the word "precise," which indicates change in policy. Because of the foregoing and many other reasons, I move the dismissal of the charge against me and demand a reconsideration of the resolution, in deference to the widespread demand of our members.

In the event that the Board of Directors deny this motion, I wish to state that I am here dealing only with the charges made by Mrs. Bromley. The additional "contempt of court" charges, 1) by Mr. Rice "that Miss Flynn's article in the *New Masses* of March 19, 1940, disqualifies her from continued membership on the Board of the A.C.L.U." and, 2) by Mr. Riis, "based on Miss Flynn's article in the *Daily Worker* of March 17, 1940," grow out of the original charge. They include sufficient separate issues so that I demand a separate trial for each if they are pressed.

* For full text see Appendix One, p. 183.—Ed.

If I am judged adversely on the first charge and expelled from the Board, I am automatically disqualified, and further trials are unnecessary. The articles in question were written in defense of myself on the first charge and even in a "capitalist court" one's defense is not immediately incorporated in the indictment, as is attempted here. It will be a nice point for the A.C.L.U. to decide to what extent these two latest charges invade my rights of free speech and free press and are a censorship of my right to defend myself publicly against public charges; as well as a further peremptory demand on March 20th, for my resignation by the Chairman, Dr. Holmes, as "the only logical, reasonable and decent action possible in the light of your two articles in the *Daily Worker* and the *New Masses*," which resignation was to be in his hands by March 25th, the date originally set for this trial.

I insist that this Board has demonstrated its incapacity to serve as an impartial jury to hear any charges against me. Mrs. Bromley, Mr. Rice, Mr. Riis and Dr. Holmes cannot surely qualify since they have assumed the roles of complainants. It is inappropriate for those who voted for the resolution to act as my jury. Dr. Holmes is doubly disqualified by his statement that I am "*a symbol of difficulties*" and that my resignation— "requested and refused—would go far to resolve them."

It is fortunate that even the "capitalist courts" do not throw one in jail as "a symbol of difficulties" during strikes or war periods! It is a neat suggestion, smacking of totalitarianism, I submit, which would be very helpful to Ford, Girdler and Co. I would ask to include here, as part of the trial record, the names of all persons who voted for the motion demanding my resignation and insist that they thereby disqualified themselves from serving as an impartial trial jury on this charge.

In view of the above, I object to the "majority" who passed the resolution, who also demanded my resignation and accepted these various charges against me, now trying what is in effect their own case against me. I challenge their impartiality and demand a trial procedure which will guarantee me a fair trial and a just decision from impartial judges. I demand the kind of trial the A.C.L.U. has insisted upon for the persons it defends.

Lastly, I protest against all attempts at "star chamber" proceedings. I see no good reason why due publicity as to time and place, and the presence of any members of our organization should not have been welcome. I request rulings now on this procedure and that a trial board be selected; that a stenographic record be kept of our proceedings; and that a decision be rendered officially on each point thus far raised; and I record my intention to appeal from any adverse decisions to whatever legal agencies of our organization and elsewhere I deem appropriate, so that I may protect my rights as a charter member of the A.C.L.U. and a member of the Board of Directors re-elected in 1939 to a three-year term and known then to all concerned to be a member of the Communist Party of the U.S.A.

(When Miss Flynn had reached the end of paragraph 3 of page 3,* she was interrupted by Mr. Finerty, as follows:)

Mr. Finerty: I would move now, as I see from Miss Flynn's statement that she has finished her challenge to the procedure, that her objection to the procedure be overruled, but that Miss Flynn be granted the right to incorporate in the record the matter she specifies.

Chairman Holmes: Do you desire to continue your statement to the end, Miss Flynn?

Miss Flynn: No, that covers procedure; you are right, Mr. Finerty. I enter then into my defense on the—well, it is all defense, but I enter into the specific charges.

Mr. Fraenkel: Mr. Chairman, in the question on procedure, there are really two elements: one is a challenge to the

* This refers to the original pagination of Miss Flynn's defense, which is continued on page 99.—Ed.

charge—the sufficiency of the charge—and one is a challenge as to the method of trial. I take it that Mr. Finerty is referring only to the second?

Mr. Finerty: No, my motion is to all grounds of challenge to procedure.

Mr. Fraenkel: If that implies the sufficiency of the charge, I think it should be separately considered.

Mr. Finerty: I would prefer to submit my motion on the grounds specified.

Mr. Fraenkel: Then I move an amendment to Mr. Finerty's motion, that the Board consider now only the questions raised by Miss Flynn as to the method of conducting this trial, not as to the sufficiency of the charge itself—on the ground that that is the basic issue, which should be considered separately and apart from anything dealing with procedure as such.

Chairman Holmes: I assume this is interpretation of the motion.

Mr. Fraenkel: Mr. Finerty has refused my interpretation, and I move an amendment.

Mr. Ernst: I want to second Mr. Finerty's motion, so that you have a motion before you.

Chairman Holmes: The motion is duly seconded. Do you offer your statement as an amendment, Mr. Fraenkel?

Mr. Fraenkel: Yes.

Mr. Lamont: I second it.

Mr. Fraenkel: It seems to me inconceivable that we should vote at the same time on matters relating to the form of trial and the very matter we are here to decide—the sufficiency of the charges.

Mr. Finerty: May I explain that we are not voting on the sufficiency of the charge? We are voting on Miss Flynn's objection to the procedure—the formulation of the charge and the method of the trial. Personally, I am inclined to vote

51

against the charge itself, so that my motion is merely to clear the way to a vote after the evidence is presented on the merits.

Mr. Fraenkel: Why don't you accept my amendment to get rid of the procedure?

Mr. Finerty: Because I see no distinction.

Mr. Frank: I was going to ask what the distinction is. I took it for granted he was not including in the motion the substance of the charge.

Mr. Fraenkel: I asked him whether he meant to include any challenge on Miss Flynn's part to the sufficiency of the charge.

Mr. Finerty: No, certainly not.

Mr. Fraenkel: He misunderstood me. It's clear, then.

Chairman Holmes: You withdraw the amendment?

Mr. Fraenkel: Yes. It is dealing only with Miss Flynn's challenge to procedure as such.

Chairman Holmes: We now have a motion before the house, as I understand it, that the Chair make a ruling on Miss Flynn's objections to the methods of procedure here tonight; and that has been seconded.

Mr. Lamont: I thought, Mr. Finerty, that you were referring to everything Miss Flynn had read so far.

Mr. Finerty: Only to the challenge to procedure.

Mr. Isserman: As I heard Miss Flynn read her reply, it seemed to me that her objections to the procedure were of several different kinds, and I think that we should take each objection up separately and rule on it. I should like at this time to amend the motion—

Chairman Holmes: May I suggest that if this motion is passed, the Chair would follow exactly that suggestion of ruling on each item of objection.

Mr. Isserman: The motion calls for a blanket ruling, and I should like to amend it so that the Chair would be empowered to follow the procedure suggested by the amendment.

Chairman Holmes: Is that satisfactory to Mr. Finerty?

Mr. Finerty: No, because in my opinion none of the grounds of objection to procedure is valid. The objections to the merits still remain. It would be very difficult to separate the various grounds in Miss Flynn's objections. I think all the objections, as far as procedure is concerned, are invalid; and that is the basis of my motion.

Chairman Holmes: Is Mr. Isserman's amendment seconded?

Mr. Greene: I second it.

Mr. Bingham: In the beginning of Miss Flynn's statement, she said, "I move the dismissal of the charges." I wonder if that is a motion that is before the house.

Chairman Holmes: The Chair will not so recognize it. No, it is not technically a motion.

Mr. Fraenkel: That is the substance—

Chairman Holmes: Are you ready for the question?

Mr. Seymour: I should like to understand this: If we accept this amendment, will Mr. Isserman or someone else, on Miss Flynn's behalf and with her approval, then formulate the objections which she is making so that we can then have a ruling on each one?

Chairman Holmes: The Chairman would so request for his own help, if nothing else.

Mr. Frank: It would seem to me that the proper method and the simplest method would be for the Chair to rule on those objections as a whole, if he sees fit and if he thinks they are all unsupportable. Thereupon, if anybody wants to appeal from the Chair's ruling on any specific point, he can raise that particular point. That is the simplest way.

Chairman Holmes: My own feeling, when Mr. Finerty made the motion, was that it was not necessary, because if Miss Flynn asked for a ruling, I would give it.

Mr. Finerty: No ruling had been asked for. That is what I wanted to call attention to.

Chairman Holmes: Do you desire a ruling on these objections, Miss Flynn, and, if so, can we simply proceed without putting the motion?

Mr. Isserman: Mr. Chairman—

Chairman Holmes: Will you speak to the motion?

Mr. Isserman: I don't understand the nature of your question, in view of the fact that there is a motion before you and a suggested amendment. I speak in favor of the motion and amendment for this reason, that if there is any discussion which comes out of taking each point separately, the Chair might be enlightened by that discussion. I wouldn't like to see a ruling by the Chair before there is any argument on any point. It is not the way things are done, and that is why I press the amendment to the motion.

Chairman Holmes: The amendment is now before the house. Are you ready for the question? You have heard the amendment. It provides that this motion, if passed, shall provide that there be no blanket ruling, but that each item or classification of objection be presented in order.

(The amendment was put to a vote and carried.)

Chairman Holmes: We are now ready for the motion.

(The motion was put to a vote and carried.)

Chairman Holmes: Miss Flynn, I will ask you to state, seriatim, the objections to our procedure tonight upon which you would like to have a ruling.

Miss Flynn: I think that in the first paragraph I say that I challenge the validity of this entire procedure as neither appropriate nor fair, since the resolution under which it is brought is contrary to—

Mr. Fraenkel: That deals with the merits.

Miss Flynn: I see. Maybe one of the lawyers ought to do it.

Mr. Fraenkel: I think there are only two things, really. I think one is the appointment of a trial board, and the other is publicity. I think those are the procedural—

Mr. Hays: No, there is a third: that we are not qualified to judge; that all of us, by passing a resolution, have shown ourselves to be prejudiced.

Mr. Fraenkel: That is involved in the demand for a trial board.

Mr. Isserman: I think it was inherent in Mr. Finerty's resolution—I don't recall its exact language—that the request to make these various documents and charges and motions and so on a part of the record is being granted, or has been granted?

Chairman Holmes: The motion has been adopted.

Mr. Isserman: So that wherever she asks for matters to be made part of the record, that is already disposed of, and they will be made part of it?

Chairman Holmes: No, they have to be clearly stated. I want some statement upon which I can base a ruling.

Mr. Fraenkel: Miss Flynn asks that there be made part of this record certain documents—in the first place, the statement of September, 1938, and the leaflet, *Why We Defend Free Speech for Nazis, Fascists and Communists,** of April, 1939. I put that as a motion, as a separate item first. I am moving that that request be granted.

Chairman Holmes: It is moved that this request for the inclusion in the record of these two documents be granted.

Mr. Finerty: I second it.

Chairman Holmes: This is not a ruling. This is just a motion that certain material be included.

Mr. Hays: Haven't we a matter before us as to these specific claims that we are not qualified to consider these charges? Shouldn't that be passed on first? That was the subject of the motion. The second motion has to do with evidence, and assumes that you have overruled the other motion.

Mr. Isserman: I think that is correct.

* See Appendix One, p. 183.—Ed.

Chairman Holmes: I will ask that that motion be suspended, if Mr. Fraenkel is willing, and again call for an objection upon which the Chair can rule.

Mr. Isserman: I will look for them; I heard them read.

Mr. Hays: May I try it, Miss Flynn?

Miss Flynn: Yes.

Mr. Hays: One objection is that we are not qualified to pass on these charges since we have shown ourselves to be not impartial.

Chairman Holmes: Is that a satisfactory statement, Miss Flynn?

Mr. Fraenkel: And that a trial board should be selected to try—

Mr. Hays: You can take that after. That is her first objection.

Mr. Isserman: On page 2, there is an objection to certain members of the Board. I think that should be taken up.

Mr. Hays: Take up one at a time.

Mr. Isserman: Mr. Chairman, on page 2 of the statement, in the last paragraph, I find this statement: "I insist that this Board has demonstrated its incapacity to serve as an impartial jury to hear any charges against me. Mrs. Bromley, Mr. Rice, Mr. Riis and Dr. Holmes cannot surely qualify since they have assumed the roles of complainants." I think that objection is a separate one from the one that goes to the whole Board.

Mr. Hays: Take them one at a time, according to your motion, Mr. Isserman.

Mr. Frank: Mr. Chairman, Robert's Rules, which I have bought for the occasion, contains this provision in regard to the trial of members of societies: "Members of the committee preferring the charges vote the same as other members."

Chairman Holmes: I haven't yet got a clear statement as to the objection upon which I can rule. I understand that there is an objection here, as Mr. Hays stated, holding that members of the Board who have already, in one way or another, revealed their attitude on certain points, shall not be qualified as voters upon this particular charge. Is that an objection?

Mr. Finerty: Yes, but that is a second objection. The first is to the Board as a whole, and I move that that objection be overruled.

Chairman Holmes: I don't think any motion is necessary.

Mr. Finerty: Very well.

Chairman Holmes: Objection to the Board as a whole—where is that? I haven't seen it.

Miss Flynn: Page 3, paragraph 2.

Mr. Wise: I understand the objection to the qualifications of the entire Board is made even if it is not in the statement.

Miss Flynn: Yes.

Chairman Holmes: I shall overrule that objection.

Miss Kenyon: If it is limited to those who voted for the resolution or were members of the Board of Directors at that time, that would eliminate, I think, Mr. Bingham and myself; we were perhaps the only people elected after the resolution was adopted, and therefore the only impartial ones present.

Chairman Holmes: Objection overruled. Is there another one?

Mr. Hays: The second objection is to the majority of the Board who passed the resolution—

Chairman Holmes: There was a vote taken on that. Is that a second objection?

Miss Flynn: I stated that the majority passed the resolution, demanded my resignation, accepted the various charges, etc.

Chairman Holmes: The Chair will have to overrule that objection.

Mr. Hays: The third objection is to individuals—certain individuals who have taken individual attitudes.

Chairman Holmes: On page 2?

Miss Flynn: Taken an official position.

Mr. Hays: Yes. They are Mrs. Bromley, Mr. Rice, Mr. Riis and Dr. Holmes.

Chairman Holmes: That is a third objection, and the Chair overrules that objection.

Mr. Isserman: I should now like to appeal from your decision in order to have a record of how this Board feels about your rulings. If done by way of motion, that wouldn't be necessary; but, since done by way of rulings from the Chair—

Chairman Holmes: You appeal from the ruling of the Chair on each of these three rulings?

Mr. Isserman: Yes.

Chairman Holmes: Is it seconded?

Voice: Yes.

Chairman Holmes: Is such a motion debatable?

Mr. Frank: I think not. I believe that the person who appealed has the right to state why he takes an appeal, and the Chair then states his side of the case, and then the vote is taken. That, I believe, is proper procedure.

Chairman Holmes: Do you desire to say something, Mr. Isserman, or just make an appeal?

Mr. Isserman: Yes; very briefly, I adopt the arguments by Miss Flynn, that in order for her to be properly tried on this charge it should be a trial by persons who have not evinced a personal interest in her resignation, and who have not voted in such a manner as to indicate their vote here now. I am fully in accord with her that the presence at this meeting of the Board, sitting as a trial board, of persons who have filed charges against Miss Flynn, and those who voted for the resolution demanding her resignation and who voted with the majority on the resolution, renders the Board such that it is not a proper trial body.

Chairman Holmes: The Chair, without extended argument, would have to reply that upon the basis of our own by-laws we are the only body that can properly act on this procedure and therefore are so qualified. Furthermore, ordinary methods of parliamentary procedure, as defined by Rules of Order, fully qualify members of the Board, in the judgment of the Chairman, to act upon the business that is now before us.

Mr. Riis, did I see your hand?

Mr. Riis: You did, for a moment. I was merely going to try to amend the objection to the ruling to include, with Mrs. Bromley and Mr. Rice and myself, the names of Mr. Isserman, Mr. Fraenkel, Mr. Dunn and Mr. Lamont, who voted the other way. If we are trying to be impartial, let's cut out both pro and con.

Mr. Spofford: Why slight me, Bill?

Chairman Holmes: It is hardly in order at this moment, inasmuch as there is an appeal from the ruling of the Chair on these particular objections which have been heard. Are you ready for a vote on the question of supporting the Chair on this ruling?

(The question was put to a vote and the Chair was sustained.)

Chairman Holmes: Miss Flynn, do you desire to proceed now with your statement?

Miss Flynn: I don't think that disposes of my charge that an impartial outside board be selected, or that some method— well, I should like to have a ruling on it.

Chairman Holmes: In view of the action that the Board has just taken, I will have to rule that such a motion is out of order.

Miss Flynn: It often happens in organizations, where they feel that they are not competent to deal with matters because of partisanship, that they do refer it to an impartial body.

Chairman Holmes: I understood you to make a motion.

If so, I will have to rule it out of order. Do you desire to proceed with your statement?

Mr. Isserman: Just to get the sense of the body, I appeal from the decision.

Chairman Holmes: Is this seconded?

Voice: Seconded.

(The question was put to a vote and the Chair was sustained.)

Mr. Fraenkel: Before we go on, there is the question of the record—a motion that I made, and that was suspended. Miss Flynn has asked that certain things be made part of the record. First, I would take up the statement of September, 1938, and second, the statement of April, 1939, and move that those be made part of the record.

Mr. Hays: I second that.

Chairman Holmes: Are there other items that you propose to include?

Mr. Fraenkel: I prefer to pick these first.

Mr. Finerty: I want to call attention to the fact that my original resolution included all documents that Miss Flynn asked be made part of the record, and was passed by this Board.

Mr. Fraenkel: I thought so, but some doubt was expressed later. Then I withdraw my motion.

Mr. Seymour: I move reconsideration of the earlier vote in respect to documentary material.

Chairman Holmes: Is this motion seconded?

Mr. Hays: I second it. I should merely like to say that the only thing I object to is the inclusion of all correspondence in the office, because that is obviously immaterial to any issue we are considering. When it comes to statements of Dr. Ward's or any statement made by the office or anything that could be even quasi-official, I think it should be part of the record. But when it comes to the numberless telegrams and letters we might receive containing the views of people, it can't possibly have anything to do with the issue we are considering.

Mr. Spofford: What would Mr. Hays include? I think that the office would have a terrible job if they had to include everything that has come in; you would have to print nine volumes. But there are certain documents that I have received, that came to me unsolicited, from, I think, important people like Mr. Frey at the University of Pennsylvania, who is Chairman of our Philadelphia Committee, and William Draper Lewis, and others; and those, I think, properly belong in the record.

Chairman Holmes: This discussion is in order if and when this motion to reconsider is passed. Is there further discussion of that motion?

Mr. Hays: I am discussing that motion.

Chairman Holmes: But not Mr. Spofford.

Mr. Hays: I should be inclined to agree with Mr. Spofford that certain correspondence may be admissible, and that is why I should like to take this up one by one, as to what is admissible. I would vote that anything be admitted that would throw any light on the controversy before us, but that wouldn't include all the correspondence we have received; and therefore I should like the motion to be passed, and then, when it comes to a question of admitting certain evidence, to vote on it.

Mr. Finerty: May I say—and I ought to do it as a warning to Miss Flynn—that my motion might be treated as a Trojan Horse; because, if Miss Flynn intends to appeal from this decision, in her own interests she ought to keep the record small; but we ought not to deny her putting in the record anything that is possibly relevant. Therefore, I am in favor of putting in the record anything she wants in the record, but I think it will be a tremendous expense for Miss Flynn to print any such record.

Chairman Holmes: Are you ready for the question?

Miss Lasker: A question of information. If we vote in favor of including the documents, pamphlets, and so forth, would we thereby be committing ourselves to the opinion that they are relevant to the trial?

Chairman Holmes: The particular motion is for the reconsideration of the original motion, and then, it seems to me, your inquiry would properly come before the Board.

Miss Lasker: I wouldn't know how to vote without knowing the answer to my question. If we were to include these various things just out of courtesy to Miss Flynn, I would vote "yes"; if, by including them, we mean that we therefore consider that they are relevant, I would vote "no."

Chairman Holmes: Mr. Hays, what would be your answer to that?

Mr. Hays: I would say that every declaration of policy by the Union is relevant, unquestionably; and as to whether or not other things are relevant, we would have to know what we are voting on. That is why I favor passing this motion and then deciding just exactly what we regard as relevant.

Mr. Isserman: In arguing against the reconsideration, I take this position: We are dealing here apparently with the appropriateness of Miss Flynn remaining on the governing body of this organization. It would seem to me that any expression on appropriateness, certainly by members of the National Committee, members of the Board of Directors and local committees and officers of this organization, would throw light on this question of appropriateness. I would suggest to Miss Flynn that she eliminate from her request the letters from ordinary members and contributors and all others, and that she limit it to letters and protests from members of the National Committee, members of the Board of Directors, officers and local committees.

Chairman Holmes: The motion before the house is for reconsideration of the original motion.

Mr. Ernst: I should like some guidance in view of Mr. Isserman's last statement. Do I understand that the objective is to get in only letters of protest, or to have letters either in protest or in favor?

Mr. Fraenkel: The letters that have—

Mr. Ernst: I didn't ask Mr. Fraenkel, Mr. Chairman. I should like to get from Mr. Isserman whether, in voting on this, he intends to have the record contain only the protests, or also all opinion from such parties as directors, officers and local committees.

Mr. Isserman: The only thing I am concerned with now is with Miss Flynn's request in her own defense. If she wants letters of other persons, or if somebody else does, that is another question.

Mr. Ernst: May I ask one other question? As I understand it, there is some kind of procedure that has to be taken up with the National Committee. I want to ask Mr. Frank and Mr. Hays whether, in their opinion, everything that is put into this record would have to be either mimeographed or printed or in some way sent out in full to the National Committee.

Mr. Frank: I don't know how to answer that, except that, as far as I can see, the whole matter is one that is really informal. As long as there is full opportunity of being heard, I have never before come across any reference to another committee. I think the by-laws happen to be stupid in that respect. That isn't before us just now.

Mr. Fraenkel: I may say, in answer to Mr. Ernst's last remark, that many members of this Board haven't seen some of the correspondence referred to here—much less, members of the National Committee.

Mr. Rice: Answering Mr. Ernst's question, I should like to call attention to the parentheses at the end of paragraph 3 on page 1, where it says: "(All letters, telegrams, etc., received in the office re Resolution, Dr. Ward's resignation, and charges against Miss Flynn are to be considered part of record)." It says *all* letters and telegrams; that is Miss Flynn's own language.

Mr. Isserman: That is tacked on to the letters of protest, and this is simply a note that these letters of protest to which she refers should be made part of the record.

Miss Flynn: I only meant to incorporate in my defense the letters which deal with the inappropriateness of the resolution. If somebody else wants to incorporate the other letters, that is another question.

Mr. Seymour: I suggest that most of these observations are appropriate to the question of what should be included, once this question is passed; and I suggest that we come to this question first.

Mr. Fraenkel: Call for the question.

Chairman Holmes: I think we would save time if we decided this motion one way or the other. The motion is for the reconsideration of Mr. Finerty's original motion providing for the inclusion of all these documents.

(The motion was put to a vote and carried.)

Chairman Holmes: We are now ready to consider such documents as we may desire to include in this record.

Mr. Fraenkel: May I go back to the motion I twice made, and move first that the documents of September, 1938, and April, 1939, to which I assume there can be no objection, be made part of the record?

Chairman Holmes: You have heard the motion that we include in the record the documents dated September, 1938, and April, 1939.

*Mr. Fraenkel: Why We Defend Free Speech for Nazis, Fascists and Communists,** April, 1939.

Chairman Holmes: Is this motion seconded?

* See Appendix One, p. 183.—Ed.

Mr. Spofford: I second it.

Mr. Frank: May I suggest to Mr. Fraenkel that he make the motion cover all the matters referred to which have been published by the Union?

Mr. Fraenkel: All right.

Mr. Frank: That covers everything published by the Union.

Mr. Fraenkel: I will accept that.

Chairman Holmes: That is the revised form of the motion, to include in the record all the documents published by the Union as requested by Miss Flynn. The seconder of the motion will accept that change, I assume?

Mr. Spofford: Accepted.

Mr. Huebsch: I just wanted to amend that to the effect that this should not require that the Board be put to the expense or necessity of reprinting any of the old literature that has formerly been issued.

Chairman Holmes: Is that satisfactory to Miss Flynn?

Mr. Isserman: I don't think that now, before we know what procedure will be followed here later, we should raise any question for Miss Flynn of expense.

Miss Flynn: Let me worry about that.

Mr. Huebsch: I am thinking of expense to the Union.

Chairman Holmes: Did you move that as an amendment?

Mr. Huebsch: Yes.

Mr. Fraenkel: I will raise a point of order on the amendment. It is not relevant to anything we are concerned with here tonight. We can't make something part of the record and talk about expense. That is something to be taken up when that arises.

Chairman Holmes: Mr. Huebsch's amendment provides the single reservation that the Union shall not go to the expense of reprinting any of the old literature. On the basis of that understanding, the Chair will have to rule that the amendment is perfectly relevant.

Mr. Wise: As one of the less intelligent members of the Board, may I ask what we are voting to include in the record?

Chairman Holmes: Such printed documents of the A.C.L.U. as are requested by Miss Flynn in her statement.

Mr. Fraenkel: Referred to at the bottom of page 1 and at the top of page 2.

Chairman Holmes: September, 1938; April, 1939; June, 1939; January, 1940. Those are the four documents. Are we ready for the question?

Mr. Lamont: It seems to me that the amendment makes the resolution itself a little ridiculous, because maybe we are out of these pamphlets, and then, in case the amendment goes through, we don't send them out as part of the record; and yet, the resolution says we are to send them out as part of the record.

Mr. Frank: Nothing in the resolution says they must be sent out as part of the record. As far as I can see, if the record is voluminous, all that would have to be done is to give notice that they are on file and may be looked at.

Mr. Finerty: Certainly.

Mr. Bingham: As I understand it, Miss Flynn is more interested in quoting a few sentences from these documents than in reprinting the whole material. I don't see any particular validity in the amendment since Miss Flynn would have the same interest as the rest of us in quoting only those sentences from previous documents that she considers relevant.

Chairman Holmes: Are you ready for the question?

Mr. Seymour: It seems to me that even in an informal proceeding consideration ought to be given to the implications of this motion. The question here, as I see it, is whether, following February, 1940, a member of the Communist Party should be a member of the Board of Directors, and whether

her membership is due cause for her expulsion—not what the position of the Civil Liberties Union was prior to February, 1940, on any question.

The purpose of the inclusion here is an attempt by Miss Flynn to indicate that the Union is being inconsistent. Its consistency or inconsistency isn't in question here, it seems to me. Therefore, it seems to me to present squarely the question of whether we are to have these things in here so that the Board or any other authority which considers it will take into account the question of consistency.

That may enter into the vote of individual members on the question of expulsion or suspension; that may be part of the thinking of individual members when coming to a vote. It seems to me to have no part in this record. Therefore, I should vote against the inclusion of that material, not out of politeness to Miss Flynn, who, of course, is entitled to attack the Board, as she has in the past, if she wants to; but on the ground that it is wholly irrelevant to the charge we are trying—what the Union said or what anybody else said prior to February, 1940.

Mr. Fraenkel: Those last remarks were not relevant to the amendment and the motion which are before us. I submit we vote on the amendment.

Mr. Finerty: On the amendment, I think that we can protect Miss Flynn's rights and protect the Board from any undue expense by passing a motion, by way of an amendment to the amendment or otherwise, by which Miss Flynn shall have the privilege of attaching these documents to the record —the documents that she wants.

Mr. Spofford: I second it.

Mr. Fraenkel: May I suggest that the whole question of the form which this record is going to take is something which this Board will have to decide at the end of these proceedings, because we are going to have a great many exhibits of one sort or another—some of the other charges are going to involve exhibits—and the extent to which they are to be physically incorporated in the record will have to be considered. I think it is foolish to consider them separately each time some exhibit is being discussed.

Mr. Frank: Mr. Fraenkel, may I ask whether Miss Flynn would give any assurance that, if this is admitted as part of the record, subsequently her attorney will not insist that everything must be printed in full and sent to every member of the National Committee, and otherwise claim that it was all unfair, having once admitted it as part of the record, that the record isn't being sent around?

Mr. Fraenkel: I should suppose that, as in every other case where there are exhibits, common sense would find a way of handling it.

Mr. Frank: Ah, but—

Mr. Fraenkel: I don't see that we should be called upon, each time an exhibit comes up, to make a promise with regard to that particular exhibit. I have never heard of a trial of any kind where such a request was made. If you were in a law court, the judge would laugh you out if you said, "I introduce this in the record—oh, but you must agree that if there is an appeal it doesn't have to be printed." That is ridiculous.

Mr. Frank: The other point is that a judge in a law court —and, of course, this is not a law court—the judge in a law court would consider rather hard the proposal to make a part of the minutes the opinion of everybody who has written about it.

Mr. Fraenkel: We are not talking about that, we are talking about these four documents, which are official documents of the Union. That is all that is involved in the motion.

Mr. Finerty: I think you know well enough, Mr. Fraenkel—and I want to recall this to Mr. Seymour, because, in my desire to cooperate in keeping this record small, I don't want to make a mistake—that we cannot, in deciding what will go into this record, do it on the basis of relevance. In any court, anyone has a right to make any offer of evidence he desires and attach it to the record, and the Court must certify it. Therefore I think, whether we agree with Miss Flynn or not that these matters are relevant, she has a right to offer them, and, I think, has a right to have them attached to the record. But I do think that if Miss Flynn desires to offer anything, it is Miss Flynn's obligation to supply it—the office, of course, cooperating to the fullest practicable degree. But I should like to see the matter take a turn by which Miss Flynn would be permitted to attach to the record such documents as she now asks, and that the obligation be put on Miss Flynn to supply it, the office undertaking to cooperate wherever possible.

Chairman Holmes: Are we ready for a vote on the question? We are voting on the amendment.

Mr. Finerty: The first or the second?

Chairman Holmes: The first amendment. I haven't recognized any other amendment; I haven't heard any.

Mr. Finerty: I offered an amendment to the amendment.

Mr. Spofford: I seconded it.

Mr. Finerty: My amendment is that she be permitted to attach the documents she specifies to the record, the obligation being on her to supply them—a substitute motion, if you wish.

Chairman Holmes: Is that substitute motion seconded?

Mr. Spofford: Yes.

Chairman Holmes: That Miss Flynn be permitted to attach to the record such documents—you make that blanket?

Mr. Finerty: As she here specifies in her plea, the obligation being on her to supply it.

Mr. Lamont: I personally don't see why Miss Flynn should have to go to the expense of attaching these various documents and getting them printed if they have to be printed.

I think the Union should understand that it does cost something, even in terms of money, to expel a member, and should be willing to assume a slight expense in order to be fair and to be sure that every member of the National Committee who has to pass on this should really get a complete view of the record. I see no reason for putting this financial burden on Miss Flynn.

Mr. Wise: Maybe we could ask the office how many copies of these four pamphlets they have left in stock.

Mr. Baldwin: We don't know.

Mrs. Milner: The 1938 supply, I am sure, is out of print. Of the 1939 and 1940 supply, we could have, I think, enough to send to the National Committee.

Mr. Fraenkel: May I suggest a way out of this? It has been pointed out that there are certain parts of these pamphlets which are important—not the whole. Is that right, Miss Flynn?

Miss Flynn: Yes.

Mr. Fraenkel: And I submit that those parts of the pamphlets that are important can be made a part of this record in printed form with much less cost to the Union than the discussion which has already been made part of the record about this motion, which I think should be physically stricken out and not made part of any record that remains to the public gaze. I think we would all be ashamed of ourselves tomorrow morning if we were to read it.

I move, therefore, as a substitute to everything that has succeeded my original motion, that there be physically expunged from this proceeding everything which has followed, and that there be made part of this record those portions of this pamphlet which Miss Flynn believes relevant, with the assurance that they will not be very voluminous.

Chairman Holmes: The Chair hears a substitute for the substitute to the amendment to the original resolution. Is this substitute seconded?

Mr. Hays: I second it.

Chairman Holmes: The substitute provides that all this discussion be stricken from the record.

Mr. Fraenkel: Physically expunged.

Chairman Holmes: And that Miss Flynn be empowered to add to this record such portions of these printed documents as she desires to do.

Mr. Fraenkel: With the assurance that that will not be voluminous.

Mr. Lamont: May I speak on the resolution? I oppose that resolution. I think that tonight it is not only Miss Flynn who is on trial, but the members of this Board, and I want to see everything that is said here in the permanent physical record for that reason. Therefore, I oppose the motion, both as it pertains to the remarks that have been made and as a precedent for the future remarks that other people are going to make here and that they will be ashamed of in future years. Let them stand on the record.

Mr. Finerty: What is the question?

Chairman Holmes: I think we know the question. Those in favor of this substitute motion of Mr. Fraenkel's will say "aye"; opposed, "no."

(Six votes were cast in favor of the substitute motion, and ten opposed to it.)

Chairman Holmes: The question before the house is now Mr. Finerty's substitute. Will you remind me of what that was, Mr. Finerty?

Mr. Finerty: In substance, it was Mr. Fraenkel's motion —without expunging anything. It was that she be permitted to supply for the record these documents, or any part thereof, in cooperation with the office.

(Mr. Finerty's substitute motion was put to a vote and carried.)

Chairman Holmes: That now takes the place of the original motion.

Mr. Wise: I raise a point of order. I suppose that we have lost track of our original idea here, and that was to pass on each one of Miss Flynn's technical objections.

Chairman Holmes: Those have all been overruled.

Mr. Wise: I think not, if I may respectfully differ with the Chair. She has raised an objection to "star chamber" proceedings. I think we ought to vote on whether or not these are star chamber proceedings, and whether her objection is valid. That is her last protest on page 3.

Mr. Seymour: In the interests of orderly procedure on this point, it seems to me that, instead of members of the Board generally bringing out points that haven't been passed upon, it would be more practicable to do what I suggested a while ago: to have Miss Flynn, and Mr. Isserman and Mr. Fraenkel, who have been making comments on her behalf, indicate whether it is now their position that each and every technical objection to our procedure here has been passed upon. It if has, then we don't need to pass on any others—because they are stated in various ways here. If not, let's pass on them.

Mr. Fraenkel: I am not raising any others.

Chairman Holmes: Have you any further objection, Miss Flynn, to submit to the Chair as to our procedure?

Miss Flynn: You have already ruled on that point?

Chairman Holmes: I understood I had. Mr. Wise refers to this statement where you protest "star chamber" proceedings. Do you want to press that?

Miss Flynn: If you have already made a ruling on the matter—

Chairman Holmes: I haven't ruled on that.

Miss Flynn: If you haven't made a ruling on it, I would request a ruling, yes.

Chairman Holmes: As that point, according to Mr. Wise, has not been clearly covered, I will overrule that objection and rule that this Board has full powers and full rights to proceed in the present method as provided in its by-laws, and that these are not to be considered, in any sense of the word, "star chamber" proceedings.

Mr. Isserman: To preserve Miss Flynn's objection, I make the—

Chairman Holmes: You appeal from the Chair?

Mr. Isserman: Yes.

(The question was put to a vote and the Chair's ruling was sustained.)

Mr. Hays: Before we proceed, and since nothing is to be expunged from the record, I think the record should show that some people seem to assume that whatever minutes we have on this hearing must necessarily be submitted to the National Committee if there is an appeal. I don't think the record should show that that is our position, because it is a very doubtful question. I don't think that should be on the record as a position in which we all seem to acquiesce, because I don't think that is necessarily the fact.

Chairman Holmes: You make due note of that fact, not calling for any motion?

Mr. Hays: Yes.

Chairman Holmes: Does Miss Flynn desire to proceed?

Miss Flynn: There is just one other point that I don't think there has been a ruling on, and that is my request for the inclusion of the correspondence. For the sake of brevity, meeting the objection raised by Mr. Finerty, I would be willing to confine that to members of the National Committee, active local committees and members of the Board of Directors, striking out "friends and sympathizers and contributors and members of the A.C.L.U." In other words, I would confine it to those who I consider have an official right to make such protests.

Chairman Holmes: Mr. Isserman, do you want to move that? It can properly come before the Board as a motion.

Mr. Isserman and *Mr. Spofford* (together): I will move it.

Chairman Holmes: The motion is that Miss Flynn be empowered to include in the record such letters and documents as originate from members of the Board and officers and local branches.

Miss Flynn: And members of the National Committee.

Chairman Holmes: Is that seconded?

Mr. Seymour: I don't see what proper place they have.

Chairman Holmes: Is it seconded?

Mr. Fraenkel: I second it.

Mr. Seymour: I don't see what proper place such documents have in this record. They have, again, a possible influence on the judgment of members of this Board when they come to decide what action to take, but they haven't any bearing on the question of whether Miss Flynn is a member of the Communist Party and whether a member of the Communist Party, after February 5, 1940, can properly be a member of this Board. That is the question we are deciding.

I don't know how many documents there are, and I don't suggest that my objection is entirely based upon the cumbersomeness of the matter; but why a branch in California, or wherever it may be, should participate in this judgment at this stage by having its protest included in this record, I can't understand.

It may be that members of the Board should be influenced by it; it may be that when it goes to the National Committee, in whatever form it goes, they will have to consider such matters; but they are quite inappropriate here. Mr. Finerty's observation that irrelevant matter must necessarily be included in the record is a fair criticism, perhaps, of traditional procedure, but I don't think that we ought to fall into the same difficulty.

It seems to me that on each one of these questions, what

74

we are deciding is whether these matters affect our judgment. It is quite a different matter whether we were right or wrong about that. I don't think they ought to be included in this record as matters that we receive unless we recognize that they are relevant and are matters that must be taken into account in reaching a decision.

Mr. Wise: Mr. Chairman, I agree with Mr. Seymour that they have no place as relevant material, because whether or not we are consistent is not on trial here. But I should like to suggest a compromise to Miss Flynn and counsel—

Mr. Fraenkel: No one is here acting as Miss Flynn's counsel.

Mr. Wise: I should like to suggest a compromise to Miss Flynn, that she submit a brief in which she would be privileged to take such excerpts as she may want from this correspondence, rather than burden the record with it. It will have the same effect, and it will be stipulated that the brief will be—

Mr. Fraenkel: A brief for what?

Chairman Holmes: Mr. Wise is making—

Mr. Fraenkel: On Miss Flynn's behalf, I ask Mr. Wise: A brief for what purpose? A brief is ordinarily submitted to persuade the deciding body as to the nature of its decision. My understanding is that the deciding body is going to decide here and now; so what will be the purpose of a brief?

Mr. Wise: If there is an appeal to the National Committee.

Miss Flynn: Some of the documents are parts of early records of the Union; some of them have already been sent out to members—the Meiklejohn-Parsons-West letter.*

Mr. Rice: I should like to support Mr. Seymour's position. As I understand it, this Board—and this Board alone—has the right to determine who shall or shall not be a member

* See Appendix Six, p. 214.—Ed.

75

of the Board, subject to such review by the National Committee as the by-laws provide. Therefore, every member of the Board, and every member of the National Committee, will have an opportunity to express his opinion by means of a vote. It seems to me, therefore, that any other expressions of opinion are irrelevant and unnecessary, and that expressions of opinion by other persons are wholly irrelevant and unnecessary. I therefore want to support Mr. Seymour's motion.

Mr. Ernst: I should like to support Mr. Seymour's position further on the ground that if these documents are relevant, then certainly all letters from persons in favor of the resolution and in favor of not having Communists on the Board would be equally relevant; and, from that point, you could go over very easily to the hundreds of editorials throughout the country and a general appraisal of national opinion in support of the resolution. Certainly, if letters from members in protest are relevant, then all of the hundreds of letters in favor of the position of the Board are equally relevant, and would have to be introduced on a counter-motion on the other side of the table.

Mr. Finerty: Mr. Chairman, I want to appeal to the lawyer members of the Board to exercise their legal knowledge. We have been told that we are going to be taken to court, and it is the most utter nonsense I have ever heard to suggest that any court will say that we have a right to determine what is relevant here. We are not accepting this evidence as relevant or irrelevant when we give Miss Flynn permission to attach it to the record. If necessary, we can rule on the relevance—I don't think that is necessary—but what we are doing, as I see it, is protecting the Union from any claim that they have excluded Miss Flynn from the right to offer anything she thinks relevant to her defense. The relevance can subsequently be determined. I ask that we at least permit Miss Flynn to attach to this record at her own expense—in cooperation, if necessary, with the office, and with the help that the office can give her—anything she thinks relevant to her defense. I think she has that right, and any court will say so.

Mr. Spofford: I want to say to Mr. Ernst that my understanding is that Miss Flynn has stricken out of her protest the part about "members of the Union and friends and sympathizers," and limited it to members of the National Committee and to chairmen or officers of local branches. It seems to me important that they should be included. I think we have had a good many communications that have been addressed to this Board that have never reached this Board.

Mr. Ernst: Both ways.

Mr. Spofford: Several of those have reached me within recent days. I don't know why they haven't been brought before this Board. I think that a man like Frey of Philadelphia is important, and that his statement—relative not to our resolution, but to the trial of Miss Flynn—should be incorporated in this record. I have a copy in my pocket, if anybody wants it.

Mr. Ernst: I would ask Mr. Spofford whether he means all such letters from such people.

Mr. Spofford: I would say yes, put them all in.

Mr. Isserman: There remains here the question of the appropriateness of Miss Flynn's remaining on the Board, and these letters have a distinct bearing on that question. Mr. Seymour suggested that some of us having heard or read some of these letters, they might influence us; and perhaps the rest of them might; and they might influence members of the National Committee. That seems to me a persuasive reason why they should be presented to us and to the National Committee.

Remember, too, that when this appeal, or this vote, goes out to the National Committee, they have no chance to meet and deliberate, so the fact that each member of the Committee gets a vote in the isolation in which he finds himself at some distant point is not sufficient to allow him to consider all the issues; and if a particular member of the National Committee has expressed himself on this—an action member of this group —then certainly the other members of the National Committee should know what he has to say about it.

That is why I think that all these letters, especially as now limited, are a relevant part of this record and should be included by us.

Mr. Hays: The question in my mind is: When? Over a month these charges have been pending. Miss Flynn has had an opportunity to prepare her statement and her answer and her evidence. I am willing to accept any evidence presented here tonight, so that I can vote on this question. I am willing to accept any evidence that Miss Flynn has, and I am willing for her to attach anything to her petition; but I am not willing to delay this interminably.

When I say that I am willing to accept anything, I would accept with considerable impatience a bunch of correspondence merely expressing the views of other people—I don't care who they are. Their opinions are wholly unimportant on the question at issue. You have facts here, and we are charged with the duty of deciding it; and it is just as absurd to suggest that we should take opinions from dozens of other people as to suggest that we should take an opinion from Martin Dies or President Roosevelt or anybody else.

I would regard it as wholly irrelevant, but I don't know if I would object to it if it were here. I suggest that we proceed and permit Miss Flynn to present her evidence—whatever she has. If she hasn't it, we will ask the office to bring it up here and help.

Mr. Lamont: I want to say, in reference to Mr. Hays's remarks, that since the Resolution of February 5 has been made relevant to this whole proceeding, the letters from members of the National Committee and local branches have the greatest importance concerning Miss Flynn's trial and the opinion that the National Committee may take of this trial procedure.

I want to remind the Board that in the past the National Committee has not been informed of both sides of the case in a proper manner. On the original passage of the resolution, only one side of the case was presented—a procedure which, in my opinion, was absolutely outrageous. I, for one, don't want that to happen again. I think that Miss Flynn's case should go in full to the National Committee, and that these letters which she has limited to members of the National Committee and local branches of the Civil Liberties Union are absolutely relevant.

Chairman Holmes: Are you ready for the question? The question is that Miss Flynn be empowered to add to her record such letters and documents as have originated from officers of the Union, members of the Board of Directors, and officers of local branches.

Mr. Hays: A question of information: When?

Chairman Holmes: Can anybody answer that question?

Mr. Finerty: May I say that my remarks have contemplated not that it would delay action tonight, but that Miss Flynn might, as a matter of information or the making of a full record here, as she pleases, attach those for the consideration of the National Committee or anybody else.

Mr. Hays: Are you suggesting, then, that we decide this question tonight and that afterwards evidence be put in?

Mr. Finerty: I don't care; I agree with you and Mr. Seymour that it won't affect my judgment in the least.

Chairman Holmes: So far as I can make out in this discussion, the resolution simply means that there is a record here tonight of this meeting and that there may be attached to that record that we are now writing here such letters and so forth as Miss Flynn desires to attach.

Mr. Spofford: And that members of the National Committee receive those.

Mr. Finerty: No—

Mr. Hays: What purpose is there in attaching them if

our decision is made without them? It is a preposterous position.

Chairman Holmes: I don't know.

Mr. Lamont: This decision is automatically subject to the approval of the National Committee; it seems to me the Board forgets that. There is no "if" about an appeal. It goes to them. Nobody has to move it; it goes to them.

Chairman Holmes: This whole record, you mean, that we are writing tonight is going to the National Committee?

Mr. Baldwin: That is not the way we do business. The Board decides separately how the National Committee shall be polled, and what shall be sent to them. That comes afterwards.

Mr. Fraenkel: We have never had a record before.

Chairman Holmes: The motion is before the house.

Mr. Isserman: A point of order! All right, if we proceed to the motion, I won't make my point.

Chairman Holmes: Is there any further discussion on this motion? I think the motion is clear.

Mr. Hays: May we have the motion again? It isn't clear.

Chairman Holmes: That Miss Flynn be empowered to add to the record we are writing here tonight such documents as originate from the officers of this Board, members of the Board of Directors, and officers of local groups.

Mr. Finerty: And may I ask if Miss Flynn will agree that the absence of those documents from the record tonight—her failure to offer them here tonight—shall not be a ground of objection to any action the Board may take tonight on the charges?

Mr. Nunn: We have seen those records; they have been read. Despite the remarks that have been made during this entire controversy, we have been bored to death with those records—the letters that have come in from all sorts of people, including a whole flock of postal cards that arrived. I see no reason at all why we should at this moment decide that a great deal of stuff that we haven't got here tonight, but that we have seen and looked at and had the office digest for us and had reports on, should clutter up this record.

Chairman Holmes: Miss Flynn, the question has been asked whether you would raise an objection based on the fact that these documents are physically not here tonight.

Miss Flynn: Mr. Isserman suggests that the point is if the members know the material that I refer to. I had rather assumed that most of the members do know the material I refer to.

Mr. Finerty: Certainly.

Miss Flynn: The Meiklejohn-Parsons-West letter; Dr. Ward's resignation; various resolutions that have come in from active local committees; Miss Van Kleeck's letters—documents that have been, I presume, known to members of the Board. I know of them; therefore they should know of them. Most of them have either been right here or have gone out from the office.

Chairman Holmes: The Chairman would be glad to have this motion put, if there is no further discussion.

Mr. Hays: That raises a very interesting question. I, as a lawyer, would not take responsibility for any of our proceedings if any of the evidence that is to be produced here either as a matter of pleading or as a matter of evidence isn't here tonight. I insist that when we vote on this motion we have in mind Miss Flynn's right to present anything she chooses tonight, and then we pass on it. There has been plenty of time to meet these charges, and I say that, instead of passing on a general motion, we proceed; and when Miss Flynn has anything to produce, we determine whether it is relevant or not.

Miss Flynn: I haven't had access to all of the material at the office. I don't know whether there are at the office more actions by local committees than I am aware of. I could submit what I happen to have copies of.

Mr. Isserman: If I thought that Miss Flynn were trying to make these documents part of the record primarily for use elsewhere, I would not support her motion to include them in this record. I believed that they would be part of the record so that the members of the Board here would consider them in their deliberations.

Chairman Holmes: Tonight?

Mr. Finerty: They can't.

Mr. Isserman: Whenever they decide this question.

Chairman Holmes: That is tonight.

Mr. Isserman: I don't know if you will be ready. If you are, you can decide it. My support of this motion is based upon the fact that if she wants these documents as part of the record, she wants them because she wants the Board to consider them.

Chairman Holmes: Do I understand that there is any proposal to extend this meeting beyond tonight?

Mr. Isserman: I don't know. A judge never asked me that before.

Chairman Holmes: I think it is quite important.

Mr. Hays: If you pass a motion of that kind, there will be good reason for extending it beyond tonight. I suggest that we proceed, and that when Miss Flynn has evidence to produce, she produce it.

Mr. Spofford: May I speak to the motion?

Chairman Holmes: This discussion is continuing for a very long time.

Mr. Spofford: I don't mean to take up time, but I should like to be clear about this. My understanding is that we act tonight and that our action then goes to the National Committee.

Chairman Holmes: It does.

Mr. Spofford: Therefore I think it important that the National Committee have all information they should have to come to a right decision, and I think there are a great many documents—in spite of what Bill Nunn says—that this Board knows nothing whatever about. The only reports I have had —maybe I haven't been attending as regularly as I should— have been reports about forty protests and fifty in favor and so on—numbers—and a great deal said about postal cards.

But there have been people of importance in the Civil Liberties Union who have written about this case. I am not interested in Elizabeth Gurley Flynn a damned bit, but I am interested in democracy in the Civil Liberties Union. I don't think that we, as New Yorkers, have a right to run the whole United States as far as civil liberties are concerned.

Chairman Holmes: I want to call attention to the fact that nearly everything being said now has been said before.

Mr. Finerty: I have a substitute motion. I move that Miss Flynn elect now whether to proceed on the evidence which she is now able to produce; or, if she desires to produce the evidence that is not now physically available, that she do so, waiving any request for delay in the decision or objection to the decision by the Board on the evidence physically produced here tonight.

Mr. Spofford: I second it.

Mrs. Milner: Mr. Chairman, may I answer Mr. Spofford's remarks? The Board was invited to come to the office and look over all of the correspondence that had been received on this question. Mr. Fraenkel came to my office, I gave him the use of my desk, and he did go through every—

Mr. Spofford: And Bishop Parsons and Mr. Meiklejohn, out in California—they were invited to do the same thing?

Mrs. Milner: We are talking about the Board. Mr. Lamont either saw it here or in the office. Everyone was invited at one time or another to come and see them.

Mr. Spofford: I am talking about the National Committee, not about us.

Chairman Holmes: Will you state the substitute motion briefly, Mr. Finerty?

Mr. Finerty: That motion is that Miss Flynn be permitted to present such evidence as she has physically available tonight; or, if she will agree to waive any objection to a decision by the Board tonight on such evidence as she does present here, that she then be permitted subsequently to present for attachment to the record the additional evidence which is thus specified.

Chairman Holmes: That Miss Flynn produce such evidence tonight as she can present; that, waiving all objection to any decision that may be made tonight on the basis of this evidence, she then be empowered to add to the record such matters as have been specified again and again.

Mr. Isserman: A point of order! I object to the motion on the ground that, on the face of it, it is a denial of any semblance of a fair trial to Miss Flynn if she is asked to present evidence after you have had a vote. Either that matter is evidential, or it is not. If you don't want it, rule it out; but if you want it as part of the record, put it in.

Mr. Hays: Mr. Isserman is perfectly right.

Mr. Finerty: I withdraw the substitute motion.

Miss Flynn: He is speaking for himself, not for me.

Chairman Holmes: I overrule that point of order.

Mr. Isserman: I take an appeal.

(The question was put to a vote, and the ruling of the Chair was sustained.)

Mr. Hays: I should like to make argument that, as a matter of law, Mr. Isserman is perfectly right, and it would be very dangerous to pass Mr. Finerty's resolution.

Mr. Wise: I agree with Mr. Hays.

Mr. Ernst: So do I.

Mr. Finerty: If Mr. Hays thinks we can rule out evidence now, why can't we condition the acceptance of the evidence for the information of the National Committee?

Mr. Hays: Legally, we can hear these charges now, or we can postpone them—one or the other. If we are going to hear them now, ask that Miss Flynn produce any evidence she has.

Mr. Bingham: I understand there is a distinction here between whether these letters are before the Board or whether they should be brought before the Committee in case it is referred back to them. According to Mrs. Milner, these letters have been made available to the Board, so they are substantially evidence. The real question in all of this controversy, as I understand it, is whether they are to be made available later for the assistance of the National Committee in deciding the question on appeal.

Mr. Isserman: A number of times now Miss Flynn has been asked to produce letters. We all know that those letters are in the custody of the office. Now, I should like to ask Mrs. Milner or Mr. Baldwin if the letters which Miss Flynn refers to, or the other documents that she refers to, are here; and if not, then on her behalf—because I am sure she doesn't understand the procedure—I would ask the office to produce them and make them part of the record.

Miss Flynn: I was going to offer what I have, and add to that a request that there be added by the office any similar documents which they have from members of the National Committee, local committees, and so forth, of which I may not have received copies. I don't know if that would simplify it any.

Mr. Frank: I was just going to explain this, because you probably do not grasp the points that have been made by Mr. Finerty and Mr. Isserman. It is this: You are perfectly willing to submit what you have physically here?

Miss Flynn: Yes.

Mr. Frank: And then you want to attach other things afterwards to the record?

Miss Flynn: Surely.

Mr. Frank: Now, a technical question has been raised that if that is done, and then a decision is made here tonight, a claim might be made afterwards on your behalf that we acted irregularly in that the testimony which is to be added afterwards was not here before us at the time that we made our decision.

Now, the point that Mr. Finerty raised is this: Are you willing to waive that kind of claim, the claim that we have no right to act tonight when the whole of the record—because you are attaching something to the record afterwards—is not before this Board? If you are willing to waive that right, then, according to Mr. Finerty's motion, he is satisfied to let these additional letters come in. That is the whole question.

Mr. Fraenkel: What goes before the National Committee?

Mr. Frank: That is a separate question.

Miss Flynn: I would be entirely willing to waive that on the understanding that I will get any additional similar documents that the office may have.

Mr. Frank: The same as though it is here tonight, it will go in the record?

Miss Flynn: Yes.

Chairman Holmes: You definitely waive any right to make objection on this point? I understand that you make definitely that waiver of any right to raise further objection.

Miss Flynn: On the evidence that will be added later?

Chairman Holmes: Yes.

Miss Flynn: Yes, certainly.

Chairman Holmes: On the basis that this evidence was not seen or heard by this group.

Miss Flynn: I wouldn't get anywhere if I didn't.

Mr. Hays: I make the same objection again to adding any evidence afterwards. Is there any physical reason why somebody can't go down and get the papers at the Civil Liberties Union and present them to Miss Flynn and let her present her evidence and have us decide what is material?

Mr. Seymour: Can't we cut this Gordian knot by having these papers and those that are similar offered, and rule then on whether we are going to receive them? If not, all this talk is unnecessary anyhow. If we are going to receive them, we have to find a way to meet physically the point that has been raised about presenting them.

Mr. Isserman: I should like to note my objection on the record, supporting Mr. Hays. I am not concerned with whether Miss Flynn waives this question or not. I am concerned about whether, in my opinion, she is getting the proper trial here. If she believes that certain documents should be part of the record, which means that they should be offered in evidence for our consideration, I still think we should have the documents and study them before we decide.

Mr. Bingham: Might I suggest a possible way out? What Miss Flynn is anxious to have is that these letters be sent to the National Committee in case they are called upon to decide. Why is it necessary to have them in the record? Can we not pass a separate resolution that they be included in any statement sent to the National Committee?

Chairman Holmes: That is the motion already before the house.

Mr. Bingham: No; it would not become part of the record.

Mr. Finerty: I think Mr. Bingham's suggestion obviates—

Chairman Holmes: I thought the motion was to attach them to the record.

Mr. Finerty: The purpose is the same, but his suggestion does obviate the technical difficulty that Mr. Hays and Mr. Isserman unjustifiably make.

Mr. Isserman: I don't think it is a technical difficulty, Mr. Finerty. You wouldn't want your client—

Mr. Finerty: I will accept Mr. Bingham's motion.

Mr. Rice: I offer a substitute motion, that all letters, from whatever source, containing expressions of opinion on the resolution be considered irrelevant to this proceeding and therefore be excluded from the record.

Mr. Hays: I second that motion.

Chairman Holmes: That is a substitute motion for all the motions that have been made, that all letters, from whatever source—

Mr. Rice: All letters, from whatever source, containing comments or expressions of opinion on the resolution—in other words, the material which Miss Flynn wishes to introduce into evidence—be considered irrelevant and be therefore excluded from the record.

Chairman Holmes: This motion has been seconded. Are we ready for the question?

Mr. Bingham: Is it proper to move an amendment to a substitute motion?

Mr. Isserman: Point of order! I don't quite understand the procedure here. We start out with a ruling on each point. If that is true, why don't you rule on this question, rather than have a motion? We have shifted back into a motion, which I thought was the proper procedure in the beginning; but we didn't follow that, so I was obliged to appeal from your rulings. Are you continuing that way or changing it?

Chairman Holmes: The Chair has received from Miss Flynn no objection in regard to letters, and therefore there is no ruling.

Miss Flynn: I asked for a ruling.

Chairman Holmes: A motion was presented, and it has been debated now for three-quarters of an hour, and it seems to me we are about ready for a vote. The Chair makes no ruling; I leave it to the Board of Directors. You have heard the substitute motion.

Mr. Bingham: Mr. Chairman—

Chairman Holmes: Have you anything new and original to say?

Mr. Bingham: I should like to say that, after disposing of this substitute motion, we could then proceed to move that all of these letters that Miss Flynn requests be sent to the National Committee.

Mr. Nunn: If they desire.

Mr. Hays: That is not part of this trial, Mr. Bingham. That will come later.

Chairman Holmes: Are we ready for the question?

Mr. Spofford: State it, please.

Chairman Holmes: That all letters, from whatever source, giving expressions of opinion about the resolution be deemed to be irrelevant and excluded from the record. Is that right, Mr. Rice?

Mr. Isserman: I thought Mr. Rice had specifically in mind the documents that Miss Flynn referred to, and was not talking about any others.

Mr. Rice: My motion has been correctly stated by the Chair.

Mr. Lamont: All documents.

Mr. Isserman: Point of order! As the motion is now framed, it is not a proper substitute motion. It deals with matters entirely outside the scope of Miss Flynn's request. I think that before we talk about other letters and documents, we should vote one way or the other on the specific request she has made. She hasn't asked for all letters.

Mr. Rice: Speaking to the point of order, I say that my motion is broad enough to include Miss Flynn's request, to cover all letters and documents. It included everything that Miss Flynn asked for and everything else.

Chairman Holmes: Are you ready for the question?

(Mr. Rice's substitute motion was put to a vote. Eleven votes were cast in favor of the motion, eight opposed to it.)

Mr. Spofford: I want my vote recorded in the negative.

Mr. Fraenkel: In order to complete the record, I am going to offer certain specific documents, one by one.

Chairman Holmes: Isn't a vote in order on the original motion?

Mr. Fraenkel: The substitute carried and took the place of it.

I offer as part of this record the declaration of Harry F. Ward, dated March 4, 1940—his resignation.*

Chairman Holmes: I assume it is in the form of a motion.

Mr. Fraenkel: I offer it.

Mr. Wise: I hope it is in the form of an offer for Miss Flynn, too. Mr. Fraenkel can't offer anything.

Miss Flynn: Yes, if it is necessary.

Chairman Holmes: Are there any objections to this being received?

Mr. Rice: I object to it because the motion that was just passed automatically excludes it.

Mr. Hays: May I ask first whether it is claimed it contains anything other than an expression of opinion by Dr. Ward? Does it contain statements of—

Mr. Fraenkel: I am not going to characterize it.

Mr. Isserman: Let the Chairman read it.

Mr. Hays: May I read it, Mr. Chairman?

Chairman Holmes: Yes.

(The document referred to was handed to Mr. Hays.)

Mr. Finerty: I make a point of order that Mr. Fraenkel's offer has already been ruled on by the Board, and that all of the documents offered in Miss Flynn's statement are now excluded. I, however, should like to advise Miss Flynn that she has a right to make an offer of proof of those documents. I

* See Appendix Five, p. 211.—Ed.

assume that is what Mr. Fraenkel wants to do, and I suggest that he do it that way.

Mr. Hays: It is merely an expression of opinion. It comes within our motion.

Chairman Holmes: It comes within the motion, you think?

Mr. Hays: In my judgment, yes.

Mr. Fraenkel: The offer will be rejected in accordance with the previous motion, I assume. I am offering them with that assumption for the purposes of the record.

Chairman Holmes: The Chair will have to rule that the presentation is out of order.

Mr. Isserman: Will that go, then, for every letter from members of the National Committee, members of the Board—

Chairman Holmes: In accordance with the resolution, I would have to so rule.

Mr. Hays: All letters that are merely expressions of opinion.

Mr. Isserman: With that limitation, Mr. Chairman, I would ask Miss Flynn to offer specifically each communication received. I don't know whether they are only expressions of opinion.

Mr. Fraenkel: On behalf of Miss Flynn, I now offer a letter received on or about March 21, 1940, signed by George P. West, Alexander Meiklejohn, and Edward L. Parsons.*

Mr. Hays: May I see it?

(The document referred to was handed to Mr. Hays.)

Mr. Rice: I object to its admission.

Mr. Finerty: While Mr. Hays is reading that, may I ask if Mr. Bingham's motion now will accomplish everything you want—that Miss Flynn be given—

Chairman Holmes: Do you think that is an expression of opinion, Mr. Hays?

Mr. Hays: Yes, sir.

* See Appendix Six, p. 214.—Ed.

Chairman Holmes: It is ruled out of order.

Have you further documents to offer? Will you offer them all together?

Mr. Fraenkel: I offer a memorandum of William Draper Lewis of Philadelphia, which bears no date; a letter from Alexander H. Frey, addressed to Roger N. Baldwin, dated February 28, 1940; a communication signed by Dr. Robert Morss Lovett and certain other officials of the Union, dated on or about March 18, 1940; a resolution of the—

Mr. Ernst: May I just correct the record? "Including certain persons who are not officials."

Mr. Fraenkel: I am excluding the names of persons who are not officials.

Mr. Ernst: Not members.

Mr. Fraenkel: A resolution of the New Jersey Civil Liberties Union, dated on or about February 7, 1940, I think; a resolution of the Civil Liberties Committee of Massachusetts, enacted on or about March 8, 1940; a letter from John A. Lapp, Chairman of the Chicago Civil Liberties Committee, of March 13, 1940; a letter from Margaret Cummings, Executive Secretary of the Washington Conference on Civil Rights, opposing the resolution. No, I withdraw that last.

Miss Flynn: Is the Lake County Civil Liberties Committee a branch of the Civil Liberties Union?

Mrs. Milner: Part of Chicago.

Mr. Fraenkel: Then I offer a letter from the Chairman of the Lake County Civil Liberties Committee, dated on or about March 29, 1940; a letter from Russell N. Chase, Chairman of the American Civil Liberties Union, Cleveland Chapter, dated March 20, 1940.

Chairman Holmes: I will ask that those documents be submitted to Mr. Hays. While he is looking at them, and in order to give our stenographer, who is very tired, a brief rest, we will have a recess of three minutes.

(A brief recess was taken.)

Chairman Holmes: I have received from Mr. Hays the opinion that these—

Mr. Fraenkel: Before you rule, I should like to add for the record two letters from Mary Van Kleeck, a member of this Board, one dated March 1, 1940, and the other dated March 21, 1940; and also the letter of the Chairman of the Board and the Chairman of the Nominating Committee, dated April 5, 1940, and addressed to Bishop Parsons, Dr. Meiklejohn, and Mr. West.

Chairman Holmes: Have you seen those documents, Mr. Hays?

Mr. Hays: Yes.

Chairman Holmes: I have had the opinion from Mr. Hays that these documents which have been submitted are all matters of opinion. On the basis of Mr. Hays's opinion, I will declare them irrelevant and exclude them.

Now, Miss Flynn—

Mr. Isserman: Just a minute, Mr. Chairman. On this point, I, of course, appeal from your ruling, because I believe that all of these letters are relevant and that they should be studied by this Board and by the National Committee.

Chairman Holmes: An appeal has been made from the ruling. We will vote on whether to support the Chair.

(The question was put to a vote and the ruling of the Chair was sustained.)

Mr. Isserman: One more point on this question; I should like to know from Mr. Baldwin the names of all the local committees who have protested this resolution and/or asked for reconsideration of it. I don't know what has been offered; I should like to know names.

Chairman Holmes: That is a request for information?

Mr. Rice: I raise a point of order. That is out of order.

Chairman Holmes: I sustain the point of order. It is irrelevant and immaterial.

Mr. Isserman: Will you hear me on it first? I desire, on

behalf of Miss Flynn—and I would suggest to Miss Flynn that she repeat this question in order to complete her offer of proof. I suggest that she ask that question of the Chair or of Mr. Baldwin in order that she can note on the record the other resolutions that she wants to offer here next.

Chairman Holmes: Do I understand that this request comes from you, Miss Flynn?

Miss Flynn: Yes.

Chairman Holmes: I will declare it out of order.

Mr. Isserman: I make an appeal from your decision.

(The question was put to a vote and the ruling of the Chair was sustained.)

Mr. Isserman: I should like to note on the record that a Director of this Board was not given information about local committees when it was asked for.

Chairman Holmes: Miss Flynn, may I ask whether you are ready to proceed?

Mr. Rice: I object to that being noted on the record.

Mr. Isserman: It's true, isn't it?

Mr. Rice: It has been declared out of order. It is putting an assumption on the record that has no business there.

Mr. Isserman: It's true, isn't it, Mr. Rice? Are you ashamed of it?

Mr. Rice: Mr. Isserman might ask what the population of Butte, Montana, is, and object that he wasn't being given information that he asked for.

Chairman Holmes: I will sustain Mr. Rice's objection. The notation is expunged.

Mr. Bingham: I should like to note that I reserve the right, after the hearing is concluded, to move the inclusion of certain material that has been declared irrelevant to the record, as properly to be sent to the National Committee.

Chairman Holmes: That will be entirely in order when the time comes.

Mr. Nunn: Mr. Chairman, just because we have a stenographer who is taking down everything that is said here tonight, I should like to say for the benefit of whoever will read this record that it would be possible for any member of this Board to come forward and submit letter upon letter, resolution upon resolution, from all sorts of people—members of the National Committee, members of the Board, and other people—approving the resolution. We haven't offered that material. It could be done.

PART II

THE TRANSCRIPT CONTINUED

Chairman Holmes: Miss Flynn, I should like to ask if you are ready to proceed with your statement.

Miss Flynn: Yes, certainly.

Chairman Holmes: Have you any further objections to offer, any technicalities of any kind to be presented before you proceed with your statement?

Miss Flynn: No, not at this point; I don't recollect any.

Chairman Holmes: Will you proceed, then? You had finished the third paragraph on page 3, as I remember.

(Miss Flynn concluded the reading of her reply, beginning with paragraph 4 on page 3:*)

MISS FLYNN CONTINUES DEFENSE

Relative to my membership in the Communist Party, I desire to place on record the facts that I joined the Communist Party in February, 1937, and so stated at the next meeting of the Board of Directors of the A.C.L.U., not as obligatory but as a matter of courtesy. No objection was made then. I was assured by the Chairman it made no difference, in which the Board concurred. In proof of this, I was re-elected unanimously in 1939 to a three-year term as a member of the Board of Directors. Mr. Baldwin wrote (April 3, 1940, to Mr. Golat, Attorney, Newark, N.J.): "We have never elected or appointed a Communist to any Committee in the Civil Liberties Union, but we have tolerated members otherwise elected who became converted."

In a letter to Mr. Nicholson, South Haven, Mich., March

* This refers to the original pagination of Miss Flynn's defense.—Ed.

25th, Mr. Baldwin states: "We never originally elected nor appointed any Communist Party member to our guiding committees." I submit that these are false statements sent out from our office, in that the records of our Union show: 1) the re-election of Wm. Z. Foster, after his known membership in 1921 in the Communist Party; 2) the election of Anna Rochester, known to be a Communist Party member, and 3) my re-election, as above stated. I was never informed that I was merely *"tolerated"* as a member; that there was an "unwritten policy of twenty years past," as Mr. Baldwin now states to justify the resolution in a letter to Miss Florence Luscomb of Boston, on February 13th. He further states, "We have *tolerated* conversions among those already elected." I challenge this implication of dual membership in the A.C.L.U. of full fledged Directors and *"tolerated"* ones, as having no basis in any action of the A.C.L.U. It is merely Mr. Baldwin's attempt by specious argument to justify an untenable position. It is on a par with the equally false statement of Dr. Holmes to Miss Luscomb on February 15th, "If you knew what we have been through in recent months, how our work has been delayed, made of no-effect, sabotaged, by members of our Board who have no belief in civil liberties except from the standpoint of their own particular interests, you would sympathize with and support the action we have taken." I defy Dr. Holmes or any member of this Board to prove sabotage, non-cooperation, or delay caused by me in any meeting of the A.C.L.U. I defy them to prove any change in my position on civil liberties or my conduct in defense of them for the past three years, since I became a member of the Communist Party.

The threatened wreckage of the A.C.L.U. and its demoralization which Dr. Holmes fears, are caused by this anti-civil liberties resolution, which he defends. I am opposed to this resolution, I voted against it and will work unceasingly for its repeal as long as I am a member of the A.C.L.U. I refuse to resign because I do not accept such a "declaration of propriety" as legal or proper. I object to a "loyalty oath"; to penalizing opinion; to the injection of issues and attitudes on foreign governments and policies; to the abandonment of the honored traditional position of the A.C.L.U. and to the substitution of political orthodoxy for the political heterodoxy which distinguished our Board. The demand for my resignation is an attempt to force a minority to conform to the political view of the majority or get out. I refuse to resign because I will not be a party to saving the face of this anti-civil liberties majority nor to whitewashing their red-baiting. I am appealing to the real A.C.L.U. elements against such a demand. If this trial occurred elsewhere it would be a case for the A.C.L.U. to defend! I am fighting for civil liberties in the A.C.L.U.! This charge violates every principle we fought for in the past. Unless the A.C.L.U. returns to its original position, its future record is likely to disgrace its past. I have a moral duty, as a charter member of the A.C.L.U., to fight against this danger and to maintain my status.

A further argument for my expulsion is the accusation that I do not believe in civil liberties in a vacuum of pristine purity, but as a means to an end. This enters the realm of metaphysics. The hypothesis of what might happen to abstract civil liberties during a period of social and economic transition from a class society to a Socialist society, is certainly not a practical problem to split hairs over in the U.S.A. in the year 1940. It would be just as logical to object to Mr. Baldwin's remaining on the Board as an avowed Anarchist, because under the complete abolition of state and government which Anarchism implies, there surely would be no Constitution nor Bill of Rights! It would be equally logical for me to object to any upholder of capitalism remaining on the Board on the assumption that real civil liberties are impossible of realization under such a society, a reasonably demonstrable proposition from the 20 years' records of the A.C.L.U.! Dr. Holmes's "holy crusade" attitude is far more objectionable when it leads him to attack the National Labor Relations Board in its administration of an Act which protects labor's civil rights and right to collective bargaining, and to defend Henry Ford's "right" to intimidate his employees under the guise of free speech, than any purely hypothetical future attitude could possibly be. Mr. Morris Ernst's playing with the Dies Committee is harmful to the prestige of the A.C.L.U. Issues involving immediate struggle in defense of the Bill of Rights are our main concern, not abstractions. Strangely enough those who are most pure in their own estimation on the abstractions are the very ones who compromise most readily on the practical issues, especially where labor is concerned.

The inclusion in the resolution of "totalitarian dictatorship in any country" and the subsequent specification of the Soviet Union as such, is firstly a violation of our traditional policy to concern ourselves only with American affairs and secondly is a misstatement of fact. I consider this resolution an insult to myself and to all other members of the Communist Party who are today members of the A.C.L.U. I object to being placed in the same category with Fascists and Nazis; and the C.P. with the Bund, K.K.K., etc. I object to the U.S.S.R. being listed as "totalitarian." I offer in evidence a copy of the *Constitution of the Union of Soviet Socialist Republics* and herewith present each member of the Board of Directors with a copy, as it is evident many have never read the Soviet Constitution. The U.S.S.R. is not a totalitarian dictatorship; it is a Socialist state of workers and peasants. "All power belongs to the working people of town and country, as represented by the Soviets of Working People's Deputies." The Socialist system of economy and collective ownership of the means of life, prevails. Capitalism, private profit and exploitation, are abolished.

The U.S.S.R. is a federal state based on a voluntary association of twelve Soviet Socialist Republics; with the rights of each Union Republic guaranteed, and a common citizenship established. The structure, basis of election, term of office, powers and duties of the Supreme Soviet and its two Chambers, the Soviet of the Union and the Soviet of the Nationalities, are clearly defined. The executive and administrative organs of state authority, the Council of People's Commissars, are appointed by the Supreme Soviet. There the extension of a people's government to industry, to the conduct of the processes of production and distribution is an extension of democratic processes to the vital needs and rights of the people.

"The Electoral System is based on universal, direct and equal suffrage by secret ballot." "*All citizens over 18, regardless of sex, race, nationality, religion, education and residential qualifications, social origin, property status or past activities, have the right to vote in the election of deputies and to be elected, with the exception of insane persons and persons who have been convicted by a court of law and whose sentences include deprivations of electoral rights.*" If such a truly democratic method of elections operated in the United States, Martin Dies and others of his sort would not be elected to Congress in the South. If an equally democratic method prevailed in the A.C.L.U. I am certain I would be elected to our Board and that my accusers might not be! To identify a new socialist order, where the "dictatorship" is the majority against only such groups as might attempt restoration of the capitalist minority control, with Fascism and Nazism which are the last putrid stages of capitalism, rotten ripe for the garbage can of history, is to declare that democracy is incompatible with Socialism.

We who are members of the Communist Party repudiate the exclusive identification of democracy with capitalism. We declare that democracy can be widened, take on new aspects, become truly a rule of the people, only when it is extended to the economic life of the people, as in the Soviet Union. As far as women are concerned, the U.S.S.R. is a trail blazer for equal rights and equal opportunities. Women are elected to the Supreme Soviet in far larger proportions than women have been elected to Congress here in the U.S.A. after twenty years of women's suffrage. The attitude of Fascism and Nazism toward women is exactly contrary, driving them out of public life and forcing them into an inferior and subject position. The rights and protection of racial and religious minorities from persecution, is the touchstone of the U.S.S.R.'s democracy as compared to Germany and Italy. The U.S.S.R. guarantees and the majority of her vast population enjoy a larger degree of civil liberties than are enjoyed by the population of the British Empire, notably India, South Africa and Ireland; yet the resolution is silent on England and France in her colonial oppression and war-time destruction of all civil liberties.

The people of the Soviet Union enjoy more democracy than the people of the Southern States, especially Negroes and poor whites. One would expect the A.C.L.U. to fairly make these fundamental distinctions between a rising Socialist system and a failing decadent capitalist system, here and abroad.

I call upon the Board of Directors to reconsider this hysterical resolution, born of panic over the European war and to rescind it as inappropriate, inaccurate, and unconstitutional. I call upon the A.C.L.U. to stand four-square on its time-honored position of defense of the Bill of Rights and the American Constitution. I submit that membership in the C.P. of the U.S.A. is not incompatible with such a position, and offer here in evidence the Constitution and Rules and By-Laws of the Communist Party of the U.S.A. I gladly provide each Director with a copy, positive that the majority of them have never read this either.

Communists have been among the most loyal and devoted

defenders of civil liberties in America, as were our predecessors, the left-wing groups of the old Socialist Party and the I.W.W. The records of the A.C.L.U. abound with our names, as those who were arrested, beaten, jailed, tried, and served sentences for free speech, free press and free assemblage.

Is there any member of this Board whose record as a consistent militant fighter for these rights can outweigh the records of Wm. Z. Foster and myself, since the free speech fight in Spokane, Wash., in 1910, which was not our first arrests? Has any one of this Board a better record against war-time invasion of civil liberties and their defense for 20 years than Earl Browder? How often has Mrs. Bromley, Mr. Riis, or Mr. Rice been in jail for free speech?

Is this Board to retain its original character, where all the groups engaged in struggle were represented from Christian Pacifist to I.W.W. and Irish Republican or is it to be "above the battle," detached observers, subscribing to abstract civil liberties, graciously willing to defend the bold bad reds, but not to associate with them?

If none of the groups we defend should be represented on this Board, as is Mr. Baldwin's latest proposal to me, then no union representative, no Socialist, no Negro, no Jew, no Catholic, no professor, no writer, no preacher, no woman, should be on this Board. Even lawyers who represent us are not impartial and should be excluded. Professional "civil libertarians" without occupation, organizational or political affiliations, or definite personal views on any other subject, will be hard to find. Even Mr. Baldwin doesn't qualify! An inhabitant of another planet might!

In conclusion, to again make the record clear, I refuse to subscribe to the offending resolution; I refuse to resign my directorship in the American Civil Liberties Union, *I deem it appropriate* to be both a Director of the A.C.L.U. and a member of the C.P. of the U.S.A. I will do all in my power to expunge the offending resolution from our records, and to make the A.C.L.U. a truly democratic organization so that such disgraceful compromise and red-baiting can never again occur. I refuse to waive my full and complete rights as a Director to exercise my rights of free speech and free press when I have criticisms to make of a public policy of this Board, now or in the future.

I move the dismissal of the various charges against me and urge immediate action on Bishop Parsons's motion* to the offending and offensive resolution, which caused them to be made.

In the event that adverse decision is rendered, I give notice of appeal to the National Committee and to the membership of the A.C.L.U.

Chairman Holmes: Thank you, Miss Flynn.

Mr. Hays: May I ask Miss Flynn a few questions?

Miss Flynn: As long as we have decided to deal only with the first charge, I think that I should make a motion only in relation to that.

Chairman Holmes: We are now dealing with the first charge.

Mr. Fraenkel: Miss Flynn wants to put into the record the documents she referred to.

Mr. Wise: While Miss Flynn is doing that, I should like to make a motion. Earlier in the evening, a resolution was passed that these charges be considered separately. I voted for that resolution, and I therefore have the legal right to move a reconsideration. I therefore do so, and move that all three of these charges be considered together, particularly in view of the lateness of the hour.

Mr. Isserman: Point of order! I never knew that lateness

* See p. 217.—Ed.

of the hour was an excuse for depriving a person of the simplest elements of due process. We are in trial now. We have been sitting three hours now. This is no time to reconsider a situation which has passed and is gone.

Chairman Holmes: Mr. Wise voted for the original resolution and now moves its reconsideration. Is that seconded? I think the motion is entirely in order.

Mr. Hays: I second the motion.

Mr. Isserman: May I have a ruling?

Chairman Holmes: I rule that it is entirely in order.

Mr. Isserman: I appeal from your ruling.

(The question was put to a vote and the ruling of the Chair was sustained.)

Mr. Isserman: I will note on the record that I asked to make a further statement and that the Chairman denied me that privilege.

Chairman Holmes: What was that, Mr. Isserman?

Mr. Isserman: I asked to make a further statement and the Chair did not allow me.

Chairman Holmes: I heard no such thing. With the consent of the Board, I will withdraw the vote that has just been taken and listen to your statement.

Mr. Isserman: We have now been several hours in the trial of Miss Flynn on specific charges. I know of no procedure in the middle of a trial anywhere—either informally or otherwise—where the issues of a trial are enlarged by adding new charges. I say that the evidence against Miss Flynn apparently is in. I understand that Miss Flynn has about completed her defense—or thinks she has—and therefore I appeal from your decision and ask that the Board members seriously consider the impropriety of adding more charges.

Chairman Holmes: The Chairman altogether declines to accept this as a trial; this is a hearing.

Miss Flynn: I am sorry that the Workers Publishers

made a mistake and sent over copies of the Constitution of the United States instead of the Constitution of the Communist Party. (Laughter)

Mr. Ernst: What a mistake!

Miss Flynn: If you would like to have them, you are welcome to them.

Mr. Huebsch: I move that we accept the Constitution of the United States instead. (Laughter)

Mr. Fraenkel: The offer is the Constitution of the Soviet Union, and not of the Communist Party, which is not at the moment here.

Mrs. Milner: I have a copy here, which you may have.

Chairman Holmes: Come to order, please.

Miss Flynn: I will take this copy and put it in evidence.

Mr. Fraenkel: What is the ruling on it?

Chairman Holmes: I have ruled that Mr. Wise's resolution is entirely in order.

Mr. Isserman: I appealed from it.

Chairman Holmes: I have already taken a vote. Do you wish that taken again?

Mr. Isserman: Yes.

(The question was again put to a vote and the ruling of the Chair was sustained.)

Mr. Ernst: I want that vote recorded. There seems to be such an issue made of it that I should like to record the number of people who have voted to overrule the Chair.

Chairman Holmes: Those in favor of sustaining the Chair will raise their hands.

(Fourteen members raised their hands.)

Chairman Holmes: Those opposed to sustaining the Chair will raise their hands.

(Three members raised their hands.)

Chairman Holmes: The motion is now before the house that we reconsider the original vote, and the gist of that is that we shall proceed, after we have heard everything on the first charge, to the second and third charges. The motion is now before the house.

Mr. Finerty: I want to agree with Mr. Isserman on one point. I think it would be very bad procedure, having proceeded on a theory by which we were going to vote on the charges separately, now to change that procedure. Miss Flynn apparently is under the impression that if we vote to expel her on the first charge, we will not hear the other charges. That, however, I think, is a misapprehension. As I understand it, we will hear all three charges and take evidence and a vote on all three charges tonight. It is entirely possible, Miss Flynn, that the procedure on one charge might be held irregular, or the charge not sufficient cause, while the other charges might be sustained. Therefore, I think I am safe in saying that we will, in any event and however we proceed, hear all three charges.

Mr. Ernst: And then decide.

Mr. Finerty: And take a vote on all three charges tonight. But I think Miss Flynn could well consent now, in view of the lateness of the hour, to present all the evidence to meet the three charges, and have us present our evidence, and then take a separate vote on each charge.

Chairman Holmes: Miss Flynn, would you consent to that proposal?

Miss Flynn: No, I don't think I could do that.

Chairman Holmes: Mr. Bingham?

Mr. Bingham: I wanted to inquire what Miss Flynn's position was on that.

Mr. Fraenkel: I don't see how we will save any time by following such a suggestion. The things are separate and distinct and must be separately considered, and I agree with Mr. Finerty that it would be quite out of order—I don't mean technically, but morally, out of order—now to change what we decided in advance.

Mr. Wise: I made the suggestion in good faith, Mr. Fraenkel, thinking it would save time in this respect—

Mr. Fraenkel: It won't save time.

Mr. Wise: If we are going to debate each one of these charges, we will be here until six o'clock in the morning; but, if we debate all three, we can still give them fair and full consideration, but we can debate as to what our vote will be all at once, rather than doing it in three pieces.

I should also like to add this, Mr. Chairman, answering Mr. Isserman, that there is nothing [at] all to his point that you can't try a person on five charges or six charges instead of one. In every court in the land, day in and day out, indictments contain two counts, ten counts, and I have one with 106 counts, and that is going to go to trial and it will all be tried as one indictment. There is nothing to that legal point at all.

Mr. Isserman: Mr. Wise misses the point. My objection goes to the fact that the new counts are being added when the case is about to go to the jury, and that makes quite a difference; I think it should to Mr. Wise, too. Furthermore, my basic objection is that the reason Mr. Wise gives of lateness is the sheerest expediency, which we should not use to deprive a person of a full hearing.

Mr. Hays: Mr. Chairman, Mr. Isserman acts as though we were submitting new charges. All these charges—all three of them—were made a long time ago. There is no reason at all why we can't take all the evidence on the three charges and then vote separately on the three charges. Nothing whatever is gained by taking the evidence on the first charge, then voting on that; then the second charge and voting on that; and the third charge and voting on that. It is a good deal like charging a person with crime and leaving to the jury the first count; and then the jury comes back with their decision, and then leaving the second; and then the third. It is a complete waste of time. Therefore, I support Mr. Wise's motion.

Chairman Holmes: Are you ready for the question?

(The motion was put to a vote and was carried, eleven votes being cast in favor and eight opposed.)

Chairman Holmes: Is there anything further to be stated, Miss Flynn, in regard to the first charge?

Mr. Fraenkel: I want to—

Chairman Holmes: I address myself to Miss Flynn.

Mr. Fraenkel: Except that I offer two documents—the Constitution of the U.S.S.R. and the Constitution of the C.P.U.S.A.

Mr. Rice: I object to their inclusion.

Miss Flynn: I should like to present these—

Chairman Holmes: Do you present it to the members of the Board or add it to the record?

Miss Flynn: I should like to add these to the record, and also present each member of the Board with a copy. I haven't got the other.

(The members of the Board were presented with copies of the Constitution of the U.S.S.R.)

Mr. Rice: I withdraw my objection.

(The documents referred to by Mr. Fraenkel were received in evidence and marked Exhibit No. 2* and Exhibit No. 3** respectively.)

Chairman Holmes: We will proceed with Charge Number 2.

Mr. Hays: May I ask Miss Flynn one or two questions that concern Charge Number 1?

Chairman Holmes: It is entirely in order.

Mr. Hays: Is the Communist Party of the United States a branch of the International?

Miss Flynn: The Communist Party is affiliated with the

---

* I have not considered it necessary to include Exhibit No. 2, the Constitution of the Soviet Union, which is a lengthy document; it can easily be found in any number of libraries.—Ed.

** See Appendix Four, p. 193.—Ed.

Communist International, yes. It says so in the Constitution.

Mr. Hays: Why draw a distinction between "branch" and "affiliation"? Isn't the Communist Party of the United States a United States affiliate of the International?

Miss Flynn: It is not a branch; it is an affiliate.

Mr. Hays: Delegates from the Communist Party of the United States are delegated to the International, aren't they?

Miss Flynn: Yes; delegates from the Communist Parties of all the countries where there are Communist Parties.

Mr. Hays: Are those delegates members of the Comintern?

Miss Flynn: No.

Mr. Hays: Is the Communist Party a member of the Comintern?

Miss Flynn: You mean the Comintern Committee that is set up during the interval?

Mr. Hays: Yes.

Miss Flynn: Sometimes the Communist Party has a delegate there; sometimes not. It isn't obligatory to have delegates there.

Mr. Fraenkel: Those questions—

Chairman Holmes: Mr. Hays has the floor.

Mr. Hays: She can refuse to answer if she doesn't want to. I think she would like to make it clear to us.

Is the Communist Party of the United States subject to direction from—what is it, the Third International or the Fourth?

Voice: The Third International.

Mr. Hays: Subject to direction from the Third International?

Miss Flynn: No, it is not subject to direction; it is subject to suggestion.

Mr. Hays: Isn't it a fact that if the Third International passes a resolution as to what the Party policy should be in America, the Party in America follows that direction?

Miss Flynn: The Party in America has the right to take it up in their Party bodies and accept it or reject it, Mr. Hays. I'm sorry that the Party Constitution isn't here.

Mr. Fraenkel: We have a copy.

Miss Flynn: But it is in the Party Constitution, clearly defined.

Mr. Hays: Has the Party here ever rejected any policy which has been determined by the Third International?

Miss Flynn: I would have to look that up. I have only been a member of the Communist Party for three years.

Mr. Hays: Has it, in the last three years?

Miss Flynn: I don't know that, either.

Mr. Hays: Are the members of the Communist Party— do you know of any occasion?

Miss Flynn: I have never heard of any discussion, pro or con, on any of those decisions of the Communist International. Many of them have no application in the United States.

Mr. Hays: Is the Communist International an organization that passes resolutions determining the policy—whether it is followed or not—of the Communist Parties in various countries?

Miss Flynn: Not in the rigorous sense in which you imply, no. In the sense of suggested policy or suggested cooperative procedure.

Mr. Hays: Is there any instance that you know of where the Communist Party of the United States, in the last twenty years, has failed to follow, to carry out, a policy determined upon by the Third International?

Miss Flynn: Oh, yes, many times.

Mr. Hays: Tell me one or two.

Miss Flynn: At the time they had those so-called sectarian fights in the Party, they were turning down the resolutions of the Communist International again and again. But I am not an authority on the history of the Communist International, so that I should hardly think you could expect me to know every decision the C.I. has ever made, and what action the Communist Party of the U.S.A. has taken on those decisions.

Mr. Hays: Let me make it clear, Miss Flynn. I was under the impression that the Communist Party, a branch of the Third International, followed the directions of the Third International. That was my impression.

Mr. Fraenkel: One moment! I must protest against that question, because it assumes in it a statement contrary to what has previously been testified to, by describing it as a branch.

Chairman Holmes: Mr. Hays can ask his questions. We are not governed by rules of evidence.

Mr. Fraenkel: I don't think it's fair.

Mr. Hays: I want to know if it is so.

Mr. Fraenkel: I don't think that Mr. Hays should interpolate into a question something which is contrary to a previous answer of the witness. We are not in a court of law, but Miss Flynn has no counsel here, and she is not a lawyer, and Mr. Hays is and should know better than to do it.

Chairman Holmes: I shall rule that a member of the Board has a right to direct questions to Miss Flynn; and he may continue.

Mr. Fraenkel: As a fellow member of the Board, I ask Mr. Hays to rephrase his question by not calling the Party here a branch, when Miss Flynn has twice said that it isn't a branch.

Mr. Hays: I didn't mean to do that.

Mr. Fraenkel: That is the whole point of my discussion.

Mr. Hays: The Communist Party of America, in my opinion, is subject to the orders of the Third International. Is my opinion wrong on that?

Miss Flynn: I think your opinion is wrong.

Mr. Hays: How about the members of the Communist Party here? Do they swear obedience to the determinations of the Communist Party?

Miss Flynn: Well, I can show you my Communist Party book if you would like to see it, Mr. Hays.

Mr. Hays: I would. I would like to know whether you are independent or whether you follow directions.

Miss Flynn: I can't very well give it to you as part of the record, but I can give you a blank book as part of the record.

Mr. Fraenkel: You can read it into the record.

Mr. Hays: You can read it. I don't mind your doing it in any way. I want to know what the fact is.

Miss Flynn (Reading): "Membership: Any person eighteen years of age or more, regardless of race, sex, color, religious belief or nationality, who is a citizen, or declares his intention of becoming a citizen, of the United States, and whose loyalty to the working class is unquestioned, shall be eligible for membership.

"Section 2: A Party member is one who accepts the Party program, attends the regular meetings," and so forth.

This is the pledge that the Party members take (Resumes reading): "I pledge firm loyalty to the best interests of the working class and full devotion to all progressive movements of the people. I pledge to work actively for the preservation and extension of democracy and peace, for the defeat of Fascism and all forms of national oppression, for equal rights to the Negro people, for the establishment of Socialism. For this purpose I solemnly pledge to remain true to the principles of the Communist Party, to maintain its unity of purpose and action, and to work to the best of my ability to fulfill its program."

That is the only pledge a member of the Communist Party takes.

Mr. Hays: As a practical matter, doesn't the Communist Party expel those who do not follow the directions of the Party in their activities?

Miss Flynn: The Communist Party of the United States, naturally, like any organization, would expel those members who apparently do not conform to the wishes, the regulations, of the organization.

Mr. Hays: Well, but don't you, when you join—

Miss Flynn: It comes with rather poor grace for you to raise that point, Mr. Hays—the right of organizations to expel.

Mr. Hays: I want to know to what extent members of the Communist Party are subject to orders by the Communist Party.

Miss Flynn: Well, do you want me to tell you from my experience?

Mr. Hays: Yes, surely.

Miss Flynn: As a member?

Mr. Hays: Yes.

Miss Flynn: I have yet to receive any order from the Communist Party.

Mr. Hays: Can you tell us what would happen, or what has happened, to members of the Communist Party when the Party gives orders for activities along political lines or civil liberties lines and members refuse to follow directions?

Miss Flynn: But the Party doesn't give such orders. You are assuming orders which are not given.

Mr. Hays: What is the basis of all these purges we read about? When men are fired out, what are they fired out for?

Miss Flynn: You mean here in the U.S.A.?

Mr. Hays: Yes.

Miss Flynn: They are tried under a regular procedure and they are deemed inappropriate to be members of the Communist Party.

Mr. Hays: Suppose they don't follow the Party line? Are they then expelled?

Miss Flynn: Well, the Party line is more or less of a hypothetical line. There is no Party line in the Constitution of the Communist Party. By "the Party line" is merely meant, in rather popular phraseology, the platform and the program and

116

policy of the organization, in which the Communist Party doesn't differ from any other organization.

Mr. Hays: Suppose the Communist Party asked you to write an article for the *New Masses* on activities of the Civil Liberties Union which we all regard as confidential, would you feel obliged to do it?

Miss Flynn: The Communist Party never made, and never would make, such a request of me, Mr. Hays. Whatever I wrote, I wrote myself, without even submitting it to the Communist Party.

Mr. Hays: Well, I didn't suggest that they ordered it or suggested it.

Miss Flynn: Well, of course, your implication—

Mr. Hays: I didn't imply that. What I am trying to get at is this: I want to know to what extent your vote as a Director is influenced by the fact that you belong to the Communist Party—your vote on any subject.

Miss Flynn: I can state it this way, without your asking questions. Probably I can state it affirmatively and make the record clear. Since I have been a member of the Communist Party, I have never submitted to any committee, body, official or person of the Communist Party any of the decisions or actions or contemplated actions of the American Civil Liberties Union. I have never even discussed it with the officials and members of the Communist Party. I have pursued my independent decision on each action as it came up in this organization in the past three years, as I did in the seventeen years which preceded my membership in the Communist Party.

Mr. Hays: There was an evening when we had a meeting discussing this resolution—the resolution that it is inappropriate for a Communist to be a member of the Board. Didn't you state at that meeting that if that were passed, you felt that in all honesty you had to resign?

Miss Flynn: No, I worded it a little differently.

Mr. Hays: What was your statement?

Miss Flynn: I worded it that it was implied that I would be expected to resign.

Mr. Hays: Yes.

Miss Flynn: In other words, that is exactly why I believe you formulated the resolution in that manner, on the assumption that I would automatically be compelled to resign from the A.C.L.U. If there were no opportunity for me to fight against that resolution and to try to change that resolution, and if that resolution were binding now and in the future, and I saw no opportunity to change it—then, of course, it would be very embarrassing for me to remain a member of the Civil Liberties Union. But, so long as I see an opportunity to change that resolution, I don't have to jump out of the Civil Liberties Union just because you pass a resolution.

Mr. Hays: That isn't what I had in mind. What I wanted to know was whether you discussed the position you were to take in the Union with any members of the Communist Party.

Miss Flynn: No, I did not.

Mr. Hays: With no one?

Miss Flynn: I did not discuss it with any members of the Communist Party. I discussed it with some of the other members of the Board of Directors of the Civil Liberties Union.

Mr. Hays: I understand that.

Miss Flynn: After the resolution was passed, and after this action proceeded against me.

Mr. Hays: Do I understand that you never discussed with any member of the Communist Party what position you should take in connection with your directorship?

Miss Flynn: I have not discussed what position I should take. I don't mean to say that I haven't discussed with any Party member what position I was going to take. I haven't been moving in a vacuum, and hundreds of people have asked me what I was going to do—party and non-party—but if you

118

imply that I consulted for the purpose of arriving at a decision, no, I have not asked for orders, shall I say, or instructions or advice from any official body of the Communist Party or any official of the Party.

Mr. Hays: Then it follows from that that the action you have taken hasn't been directed by the Communist Party?

Miss Flynn: It hasn't been directed by the Communist Party.

Mr. Wise: I just want to ask two questions. Since you have offered the Constitution of the Union of Soviet Socialist Republics in evidence, Miss Flynn, I should like to ask you if you can tell me whether or not Article 125, which reads in part: "In conformity with the interests of the working people, and in order to strengthen the socialist system, the citizens of the U.S.S.R. are guaranteed by law: (a) freedom of speech; (b) freedom of the press; (c) freedom of assembly, including the holding of mass meetings"—whether or not that includes in practice, in the Soviet Union, the same comparable right that we have in this country to criticize our Executive and the heads of our Government.

Miss Flynn: Well, of course, I have never been in the Soviet Union, and it might be that some people who have been in the Soviet Union could better answer that question than I can, from practical experience. But I would say, from my reading and from whatever has come to my hand about the Soviet Union, that in those matters which pertain to their rights and their duties and their economic status and so forth —yes, they have even more free speech in the Soviet Union than we have in some parts of the United States.

Mr. Wise: Putting it colloquially, is it your opinion that in Russia you have the same right to say "Stalin is a bum" that we have in this country to say "Roosevelt is a bum"?

Miss Flynn: I don't know about that.

Mr. Wise: And the other question I have is this—

Miss Flynn: I have not been there, and I don't know that this is particularly germane to the subject, because I don't know that I am asked to defend any possible abuses or failure to enforce the Constitution of the Soviet Union in periods, possibly, of war and stress and so forth. Do you think that I should undertake a complete defense of the Soviet Union here in my trial?

Mr. Wise: No, Miss Flynn. I was just curious as to whether you had any knowledge on that subject.

The other question I should like to ask is this—

Miss Flynn: The position I take, Mr. Wise, is that whether they have or have not is not germane to the American Civil Liberties Union. It has been injected into the Civil Liberties Union by this resolution. The stigma of being a totalitarian has thereby been placed upon me. Therefore it becomes necessary for me to demonstrate that the Soviet Union is not, in my opinion, a totalitarian state. I am not attempting to say that the Soviet Union is perfect, that there are not abuses, shortcomings, that there are not many conditions which should, and could, be remedied. But I certainly am objecting to the classification of "totalitarian" as applying to the Soviet Union; and offering the Constitution and the general workings of what they are trying to achieve is a refutation of that "totalitarian" definition.

Mr. Wise: The only other question I want to ask you is this: Whether members of the Communist Party in this country are subject to discipline if they make derogatory statements, (a) about the leaders of the Party in this country, and (b) about Stalin or the other leaders of the Party in Russia.

Miss Flynn: The members of the Communist Party have a right to criticize within the organization of the Communist Party, or even outside of the organization of the Communist Party, if the activities of those leaders go outside the confines of the Communist Party—certainly. If, of course, a statement is made which is utterly and absolutely untrue, beyond all possibility of truth, that is another matter, I think. The Communist Party disciplines its members in the same sense that a trade union or any other political party or any organization does.

Mr. Wise: For expressions of opinion?

Miss Flynn: I suppose you are laying the basis for the second charge and the third charge against me.

Mr. Wise: I am not laying any basis for anything. I am really open-minded and curious. If you can convince me one way, I will vote one way; if you convince me the other, I will vote the other.

Miss Flynn: I am trying to convince you one way, Mr. Wise.

Mr. Wise: If I can explain my question and amplify it, it has always been my opinion that a true member of the Communist Party in this country cannot criticize Stalin or his policies, and cannot criticize Browder and his policies, openly and publicly and in the press in such a way as to embarrass either Stalin or Browder, and not be disciplined for it. If you say that is not so, I will accept your statement.

Miss Flynn: In the first place, it wouldn't be necessary for a member of the Communist Party. Suppose that I myself have a criticism to make of Earl Browder as Secretary of the Communist Party. I have recourse to sufficient machinery of the Party, starting with the branch to which I belong, through the section, through the county, through the state, through the National Committee, to the convention of the Party, to take my grievance, if necessary, to the largest elected delegate body.

Now, all over the country, state conventions are being held, electing delegates to a national convention of the Communist Party which will be held here on Decoration Day. That is the governing body of the Party.

Mr. Wise: What would happen—

Miss Flynn: If there were no such machinery established, then the Communist Party member would have to have recourse to outside agencies. But there is that machinery established, and the rights of members to criticize are carefully safeguarded within the Communist Party.

Mr. Wise: What would happen if you didn't go to this body of delegates, and took your grievance directly to the public first? What would happen to you as a member?

Miss Flynn: Well, it would depend upon the provocation, I might say.

Mr. Wise: Suppose it were severe—would you be disciplined?

Miss Flynn: It would depend upon the provocation.

Mr. Wise: I think that is enough.

Mr. Fraenkel: I should like to ask Miss Flynn some questions.

Chairman Holmes: You may.

Mr. Fraenkel: Miss Flynn, there has been mention here about the affiliation of the Communist Party of the United States with the Third International. How long has that affiliation been in existence?

Miss Flynn: I don't think I can answer that.

Mr. Fraenkel: It was in existence before you became a member of the Party?

Miss Flynn: Oh, yes, yes. It is a matter of many years, but I don't know accurately the number.

Mr. Fraenkel: That is a matter of common knowledge, isn't it?

Miss Flynn: Certainly.

Mr. Fraenkel: All the other conditions about which you were asked concerning the Communist Party were also in existence before you became a member of the Party, is that not so?

Miss Flynn: Certainly.

Mr. Fraenkel: And also matters of common knowledge.

Miss Flynn: Yes, certainly. It's no secret.

Mr. Fraenkel: You were asked earlier in this hearing about your having been a member of the National Committee of the Communist Party?

Miss Flynn: Yes.

Mr. Fraenkel: When did you become a member of that National Committee?

Miss Flynn: Within the last two years. I think it was in the summer of 1938.

Mr. Fraenkel: And was that a matter of common knowledge, public knowledge?

Miss Flynn: Well, it should have been, because I was the only person elected in the open convention of the Party, and not by the referendum of the district delegations, because I wasn't actually eligible to be a member of the National Committee. I hadn't been a sufficiently long time a member of the Party, and an exception had to be made, and it had to be done in open convention of the Party.

Mr. Fraenkel: Might I ask Mr. Baldwin if he had knowledge of that about the time that it happened?

Mr. Baldwin: That Miss Flynn was a member of the National Committee of the Communist Party?

Mr. Fraenkel: Yes.

Mr. Baldwin: I don't recollect it, no.

Mr. Fraenkel: Do you recollect knowing that before Miss Flynn was reelected in 1939?

Mr. Baldwin: I think I probably knew th c before 1939, yes.

Mr. Fraenkel: Now, Miss Flynn, there has been mention here about disciplinary action, or possible disciplinary action, taken against members of a party. The Communist Party is not the only political party in the United States of which that might be said, is it?

Miss Flynn: Certainly not.

Mr. Fraenkel: Are you familiar with the Socialist Party of the United States?

Miss Flynn: Yes.

Mr. Fraenkel: The Socialist Party, by the way, was also affiliated with an international body for many years?

Miss Flynn: Yes, that's right.

Mr. Fraenkel: And still is, is it not?

Miss Flynn: Yes, the Second International.

Mr. Fraenkel: And the Socialist Party also has a Constitution?

Miss Flynn: Yes.

Mr. Fraenkel: And a pledge of obedience to party principles exacted from its members?

Miss Flynn: Surely.

Mr. Fraenkel: And there have been occasions when there have been purges in the Socialist Party?

Miss Flynn: Very drastic ones.

Mr. Fraenkel: And persons expelled for not following the Party line?

Miss Flynn: Yes.

Mr. Lamont: Such as Dr. Holmes.

Mr. Hays: Don't you, Miss Flynn, make it a policy to lay stress upon the discipline of your members in the Communist Party?

Miss Flynn: I don't think so. I think non-party people make a lot more to-do about it than party people.

Mr. Hays: Isn't it a disciplined party in the sense that the members are supposed to follow a discipline laid down from above?

Miss Flynn: No, not in that sense at all. It is a disciplined body in the sense that any organization is a disciplined organization.

Mr. Hays: And no more than that, no more than the Socialist Party?

Miss Flynn: I don't think it is any more, but I would

have to go into that. I am not so sure that the Socialist Party isn't more disciplined in the sense that you imply.

Mr. Hays: I am interested also in your attitude towards civil liberties. Do you believe in civil liberties and democracy or the Bill of Rights as a way of life, or merely as a means to bring about a Soviet system in this country, a Communist system?

Mr. Isserman: A point of objection! A point of order!

Chairman Holmes: I will recognize no objections.

Mr. Isserman: I should like to state it. I should like to appeal from your decision to refuse to listen to my point.

Miss Flynn: It is a matter which relates to my own opinions as a person who believes in civil liberties.

Mr. Hays: No, but there are reasons why "Communist" is mentioned. We may be entirely under a misapprehension; I am trying to find out. I am trying to find out: Do you believe in civil liberties or merely in the use of civil liberties to change this Government so that we will have a Communist form over here?

Mr. Isserman: I want to press my objection.

Mr. Fraenkel: I should like to ask—

Chairman Holmes: Objection has been made to the ruling of the Chair. We will vote on whether to sustain the Chair.

(The question was put to a vote and the ruling of the Chair was sustained by a vote of 11 to 9.)

Chairman Holmes: Proceed, Mr. Hays.

Mr. Fraenkel: I should like to ask Mr. Hays a question.

Chairman Holmes: Proceed, Mr. Hays.

Mr. Fraenkel: Will Mr. Hays permit me—

Mr. Lamont: Will anyone else get a chance?

Mr. Fraenkel: Will Mr. Hays permit me to ask a question?

Mr. Hays: Yes.

Mr. Fraenkel: Mr. Hays, do you consider that it is fitting and appropriate, where the charge against Miss Flynn is her membership in the Communist Party, to question her about her private views?

Mr. Hays: No, I am questioning her about her views as a Communist.

Mr. Fraenkel: Then may I suggest that any questions which you ask be so phrased that there can be no misunderstanding on that subject?

Chairman Holmes: Proceed, Mr. Hays.

Mr. Fraenkel: I conceive that your last question is not properly phrased in light of your own statement on your intention.

Mr. Hays: You are perfectly right.

Miss Flynn, do members of the Communist Party believe in civil liberties and democracy as a way of life, or merely that they are useful methods to be used in a democracy towards bringing about a Communistic system and a dictatorship of the proletariat?

Miss Flynn: What do you mean by "a way of life," Mr. Hays?

Mr. Hays: I mean an end in itself—the right of liberty as an end in itself. Or do you merely believe that it is a means to bring about a Soviet system or a Communist system, and that civil liberties are useful for that purpose?

Miss Flynn: Well, I don't think that my conception of civil liberties has been changed by my membership in the Communist Party.

Mr. Hays: I am not asking you your conception. I changed that when Mr. Fraenkel pointed it out. I am asking you the conception of the Communist Party. Do you know their view as to civil liberties in the United States—whether they are merely a good method to bring about the overthrow of the Government and the substitution of a dictatorship of the proletariat, or whether they themselves are valuable as an end in themselves?

Miss Flynn: Well, I know of no resolution or official action or statement of the Communist Party on civil liberties, as you have now expressed it. There is no such statement that I know of on civil liberties coming officially from the Communist Party or expressed by any of the leaders of the Communist Party.

Mr. Hays: Isn't it a fact that the view of—

Miss Flynn: Where do you get that idea? What is the basis of your—

Mr. Hays: I think I have heard Communists time and again make the statement that civil liberties are all right to enable them to bring about a Soviet system of government, and then civil liberties will have to be suppressed until they are able to establish a Socialist Commonwealth.

Miss Flynn: Well, that is a purely hypothetical question as to a transition period, which might apply, as Mr. Frank demonstrated, to many who are not Communists, and who are also members of this Board.

Mr. Hays: Isn't that the position, though, of the Communist Party—that civil liberties are very valuable in the United States in order to bring about a situation where Communists can control the Government and set up a dictatorship of the proletariat, perhaps as a temporary measure?

Miss Flynn: Your statement is an absolutely inaccurate statement of the position of the Communist Party. The Communist Party does not want to control the Government. The Communist Party is not setting out to set up a dictatorship in the United States of America. The Communist Party is trying to bring about the control by the people of this country of the Government, and the setting up of Socialism in this country, and there is the possibility implied in all of the literature of the Communist Party that Socialism is possible under democracy and democratic forms in the United States of America.

Mr. Hays: But there must be a transition period through a dictatorship of the proletariat?

Miss Flynn: May be, not must be. There may be.

Mr. Hays: All right.

Chairman Holmes: Are you through, Mr. Hays? Mr. Finerty has been calling for the floor.

Mr. Hays: Yes.

Mr. Finerty: I just wanted to ask you, Miss Flynn, if you knew of any party in the United States other than the Communist Party that requires a pledge from its membership.

Miss Flynn: I think the Socialist Labor Party does; I think the Socialist Party does—I don't know; the Labor Party certainly does.

Mr. Finerty: A pledge?

Miss Flynn: The American Labor Party.

Mr. Finerty: I happen to be a member, and I have never signed a pledge.

Miss Kenyon: I, neither.

Mr. Dunn: The Woman's Christian Temperance Union does.

Miss Flynn: My son was expelled from the American Labor Party Club because he refused to accept the resolution on the Soviet Union and Finland; so that is by implication a pledge, is it not?

Miss Kenyon: I refused also to sign the same thing and was not expelled.

Mr. Finerty: May I ask you this? Referring to the pledge which you, as a member of the Communist Party, have taken, I should like to ask you what interpretation you make on this point—

Miss Flynn: As a matter of fact, I didn't take this pledge, Mr. Finerty, because this was written into the Constitution subsequent to my joining the Communist Party.

Mr. Finerty: But, of course, morally, in remaining a member of the Party, you consider yourself bound by the pledge?

Miss Flynn: Yes—just to clear the record. Certainly, I would take the pledge—gladly.

Mr. Finerty (Reading): "For this purpose, I solemnly pledge to remain true to the principles of the Communist Party, to maintain its unity of purpose and of action, and to work to the best of my ability to fulfill its program."

Now, do you believe that consistently with that pledge, and assuming the Communist Party laid down a program, you could remain a member of the Communist Party or keep your pledge if you refused to follow that program?

Miss Flynn: As the program is laid down, I do subscribe to it and do consider it consistent with being a member of the A.C.L.U.

Mr. Finerty: I am not asking whether you consider it consistent; it may be. But, whatever the program of the Communist Party, whatever it may be, so long as you are a member of that Party, you are pledged to follow that program—whether it is consistent with the Civil Liberties Union or anything else?

Miss Flynn: That is true of any organization where you have majority rule, thorough discussion, and thorough difference of opinion, and finally a decision as to what the majority position is. Then you reserve the right, as a minority, to continue to work to change the position. But you don't—well, you resign otherwise.

Mr. Finerty: Let me ask you this—

Miss Flynn: Of course, I understand your analogy is that therefore I should do the same thing in the A.C.L.U.

Mr. Finerty: No, that isn't. I am going to tell you what my analogy is right now. I should like to know whether, if the Communist Party should adopt as its program the suppression of civil liberties, you would, consistently with that pledge, remain a member of the Civil Liberties Union.

Mr. Fraenkel: I object to that question. I think it should be put in a different form.

Chairman Holmes: The Chair is not going to recognize any objections to questions.

Mr. Fraenkel: I will again ask Mr. Finerty—

Mr. Finerty: No, I am not debating with you, Mr. Fraenkel.

Miss Flynn: That is a hypothetical question, like "Do you still beat your wife? Answer yes or no." It is purely a hypothetical question, and certainly I would be confronted with either resigning from the Communist Party or resigning from the Civil Liberties Union.

Mr. Finerty: That is the correct answer.

Miss Flynn: But that position does not exist at the present time, and therefore is not germane to the issue.

Mr. Lamont: I think I can throw some light on this, but first I want to ask Mrs. Bromley something that is puzzling me: Why do you consider membership in the Communist Party and the National Committee enough of a charge for Miss Flynn to be expelled from this Board?

Mrs. Bromley: Because of the very clear phrasing of our Resolution of February 5. Having voted for that resolution, I think this is the only consistent procedure for us to follow.

Mr. Lamont: Just in reference to that resolution?

Mrs. Bromley: Yes; I thought it through then to my own satisfaction. The Board adopted it—a majority of the Board adopted it.

Mr. Lamont: I just want to make a statement on party discipline in the United States which is—

Mr. Ernst: May we finish asking Miss Flynn questions first?

Mr. Lamont: I will ask Miss Flynn some questions.

Are you aware, Miss Flynn, that Dr. Holmes was expelled from the Socialist Party for not following the party line?

Miss Flynn: I have a recollection of it, yes.

Mr. Lamont: It is true. Are you aware that my wife, Margaret Lamont, is a member of the Socialist Party?

130

Miss Flynn: Yes.

Mr. Lamont: Are you aware that, three weeks ago, she was forbidden by the Socialist Party to go on a committee to defend the civil liberties of the persons who picketed the French and other Embassies—what were they?

Voices: The French Embassy.

Mr. Lamont: Yes, the French Embassy.

Miss Flynn: I didn't know it, no.

Mr. Lamont: Are you aware that one week ago she was forbidden by the Socialist Party to make a speech showing the progress of women in the Soviet Union?

Miss Flynn: No.

Mr. Lamont: Those are all my questions for the present.

Mr. Isserman: Do you know, Miss Flynn, of any members of this Board who are members of the Socialist Party?

Mr. Seymour: I object on the grounds—

Mr. Isserman: I thought no objections—

Chairman Holmes: I am not going to recognize any objections to questions.

Miss Flynn: I suppose it is common knowledge that Mr. Thomas is; I don't know about any others.

Mr. Wise: I move the question be tabled.

Chairman Holmes: Proceed, Mr. Isserman.

Mr. Isserman: I call your attention to the objects of the American Civil Liberties Union, as expressed in Section 2 of the by-laws, which reads as follows: "To maintain throughout the United States and its possessions the rights of free speech, free press, free assemblage and other civil rights, and to take all legitimate action in furtherance of such purposes." And I ask you whether there is anything in your membership or affiliation with the Communist Party which prevents you from whole-heartedly supporting this item of our by-laws.

Miss Flynn: There is not.

Mr. Isserman: No other questions. Yes, I have one more,

131

please; I have one to ask of Mrs. Bromley. Mrs. Bromley, do you know of any action taken by Miss Flynn as a member of the Civil Liberties Union Board or otherwise, prior to the date of the filing of your charge in this case, which, in your opinion, made her an improper member of this Board?

Mrs. Bromley: Mr. Isserman, my charge against Miss Flynn is based not upon her personal actions, but upon her membership in the Communist Party.

Mr. Isserman: Is the answer "No," then, to the thing I asked you?

Mrs. Bromley: Yes.

Mr. Ernst: I should like to ask Elizabeth just one question. In the light of the Civil Liberties Union's position that people should not be barred from this country because of political belief, and in the light of your pledge to the Communist Party, could you state how you would vote on a question such as, for example, the position of the Union with respect to opposing the barring of the admission of Trotzky to the United States? Could you state it? If you can't—why, that is the end of the question.

Miss Flynn: Well, that just reminds me that Mr. Riis wrote a letter to Mrs. Lavinia Dodd in which he said I had already taken that position; I have no recollection or knowledge of having taken that position.

Mr. Ernst: I didn't say you took any. I knew you were absent at the meeting.

Miss Flynn: Opposing free speech for Trotzky? I didn't even know that Trotzky was up for issue as a free speech case before the Civil Liberties Union, and I don't remember having been called on to vote on it. You mean on a question of political asylum, coming into the United States?

Mr. Ernst: Yes.

Miss Flynn: I don't think the Communist Party would give me any instructions on that matter whatsoever, any more than on the matter of the Beal case. I have never opposed any action on the part of this Board, or members of this Board, to secure the release of Fred Beal from prison; and I say now that I did not oppose the legal admission of Trotzky into the United States.

Mr. Ernst: So you would vote for the admission of Trotzky to the United States?

Miss Flynn: I don't say I would vote for it. I said I would not oppose it, Morris. One may refrain from voting on a particular issue that he is not very keen on, you know. I don't say I would vote in favor of it, but I wouldn't oppose it.

Mr. Ernst: You would not vote in favor?

Miss Flynn: Many members of this Board refrain from voting on things they are not interested in. I have seen that many, many times. Do you assume I must vote affirmatively?

Mr. Ernst: No, I assume your position is that you wouldn't be interested in the Trotzky matter, and therefore wouldn't vote in favor.

Miss Flynn: There are a lot of people about whom I wouldn't be interested in their coming into the United States, but I wouldn't oppose their theoretical right to come in.

Mr. Bingham: Is it in order at this point to introduce a resolution on the action we should take on this charge?

Chairman Holmes: No, we will proceed next to Charge Number 2.

Mr. Fraenkel: I have a motion to make.

Mr. Lamont: I have some more questions to ask, but if you want to make your motion—

Mr. Fraenkel: No.

Mr. Lamont: Has the Communist Party changed its attitude towards civil liberties in America since the pact between the Soviet Government and the German Government?

Miss Flynn: No, it has not. In fact, we have been compelled to fight all the harder for civil liberties, I should say.

Mr. Lamont: Are you aware that Marx once made a speech in which he said that, in England and the United States, it seemed to him there was a very good chance of achieving a Socialist society through democratic procedures; and, in view of that speech, wouldn't you say that it was the opinion of the Communist Party that every effort should be made to achieve a Socialist society through ordinary civil liberties?

Miss Flynn: Certainly.

Mr. Lamont: And that is its present program?

Miss Flynn: That is the present program of the Communist Party, and I regret exceedingly that I didn't have enough copies of the Constitution to give all the members of the Board.

Mr. Lamont: Have you specialized in the defense of the Soviet Union, or anything of that sort?

Miss Flynn: No, I have not. I have specialized, if there is such a thing as specializing, in the defense of civil liberties, I should say, for Communists and others over a period of many years.

Mr. Lamont: Don't you think—

Miss Flynn: I don't think anybody here will dispute that.

Mr. Lamont: Don't you think it is a little odd that since this Resolution of February 5 is particularly aimed at those who sympathize with the so-called totalitarian government of the Soviet Union, the one person on the Board—namely, myself—who has specialized on the educational work concerning the Soviet Union over the last seven years should not have been brought to trial, rather than yourself? Don't you think that it is rather odd that since in the last week or two I have published articles reaffirming my general sympathy with the Soviet Union and the progress that has been made there, I, as the outstanding sympathizer with the Soviet Union on this Board, should not have been brought to trial, rather than yourself?

Miss Flynn: Well, I should think, if this resolution means what it says, that you should be brought to trial, Mr. Lamont —although I am not ready to prefer the charges against you.

Chairman Holmes: Are we ready to proceed with the second charge?

Mr. Fraenkel: I don't know if it is in order, but I now move to dismiss the first charge on the ground that the charge itself is insufficient to justify expulsion, and that none of the evidence here produced justifies it.

Chairman Holmes: I should like to postpone consideration of that motion until after we have heard the second and third charges, in accordance with the action taken by the Board of Directors.

Mr. Isserman: I should like to make a similar motion. Will that be postponed also?

Chairman Holmes: Yes.

Mr. Wise: I make another motion, Mr. Chairman. In the interests of a fair trial for Miss Flynn, I move we adjourn. That is a motion that doesn't have to be seconded, and doesn't have to be voted on, but I make it on this record. It is now twenty minutes to twelve.

Mr. Hays: What of it?

Mr. Wise: We have two more charges to hear. I don't think we should hurry through them.

Mr. Ernst: They won't take five minutes.

Mr. Wise: I don't know how long they will take.

Chairman Holmes: Is that motion seconded? (No response) The Chair hears no second. We will proceed.

Mr. Wise: May the record show that I withdraw at this point?

Chairman Holmes: Do you have to?

Mr. Wise: Yes.

(Mr. Wise left the meeting.)

Chairman Holmes: Mr. Rice, are you ready to present Charge Number 2?

Mr. Rice: Yes. My charge is based on an article by Miss

Flynn in the *New Masses* of March 19, 1940, entitled, "Why I Won't Resign from the A.C.L.U." I should like to say for the record that my charge has nothing to do with the February Resolution. It has nothing to do with Miss Flynn's membership in the Communist Party. It is based entirely on what might be called moral or ethical grounds—or human relations, if you want to put it that way.

I want to make briefly another point which I think is important for the record. An attempt has been made by Miss Flynn and by one or two other members of the Board to treat this proceeding as though it were (a) a legal trial of a person under indictment for a crime, and (b) as though it were the impeachment of a member of a legislative body, let's say.

I think that is an entirely false assumption, and I think a great deal of the argument and discussion tonight has been based upon that false assumption, and that the record is going to make something appear which is not a fact. Miss Flynn is not charged with a crime. She is not under indictment. All this talk about juries and judges and so on is utterly irrelevant and has no bearing upon the proceedings at all.

The same thing is true of the attempt to treat this as though it were the impeachment proceeding of a person who was elected to public office and who is a member of some governmental agency. That is not true, either.

This has a direct bearing on my charge, as I will show you in a moment. Miss Flynn is charged, as I understand it— and specifically with relation to my charge—with being no longer qualified to sit on this Board. In other words, this, in my opinion, has none of the aspects of a trial or impeachment proceeding. It is simply the action of a group of people associated in a particular kind of work, deciding whether or not another person is qualified to continue in the performance of that work.

This is not a public organization. It is not an elected

body. It is a self-constituted organization, a voluntary association of persons who presumably have one common interest— the preservation of civil liberties. In any such association, the essential thing that makes it tick is their esprit de corps. It is like-mindedness, it is consciousness of kind, it is a common interest for a particular objective.

It seems to me that is the sine qua non of any membership in such a Board as this is. We have no other responsibility other than to ourselves and to each other and to those who believe as we do, and to the principles in which we are interested—namely, the preservation of civil liberties.

I am not going to read the entire article by Miss Flynn.

Mr. Baldwin: It was sent to all members of the Board.

Mr. Rice: I assume you don't all want to listen to it. I am offering it as evidence, as part of the record. I will confine my reading to the last five or six sentences—the part of the last paragraph in which Miss Flynn, after making various charges against the A.C.L.U. as a body and certain of its directors and officers, says:

"The A.C.L.U. directors have become class conscious. When labor was weak they could afford to be the benign, detached liberals demanding the rights of labor. But labor is strong and powerful today. It needs no wet nurses! These pseudo-liberals take fright at the giant on the horizon which points the possible future everywhere—the Soviet Union. I don't mind being expelled by this kind of people. I don't belong with them anyhow. I'll fight them to expose them, not from a desire to associate with them any longer. Labor can defend its own civil liberties—so can the Communists, without the A.C.L.U."

That is my entire case. I submit that the author of those lines, appearing in a publication that has general circulation, automatically disqualifies herself from further membership on this Board.

Chairman Holmes: Miss Flynn?

Miss Flynn: I didn't expect to have to go into the proof of the subject-matter of the articles. That is considerable of a task, and I don't know whether I am quite prepared to do it at this moment. That is what you now call upon me to do.

Mr. Rice: No, my charge doesn't relate to the subject-matter of the article; it relates merely to the attitude expressed in the sentences I have read.

Miss Flynn: Then I should say, if it refers to the attitude, that you have to take into consideration considerably the circumstances which produced the attitude—namely, a resolution was passed by this Board and given the most unseemly publicity, with interpretations by both the Chairman and Mr. Baldwin, and with virtually no interpretations of the minority group reaching the public whatever. There was immediately an acclaim in all of the—what we call the "bourgeois" papers—praising the action of the American Civil Liberties Union. There was no channel through which any of us could voice our protest, except such an organ as the *New Masses*.

There are people on this Board whom I consider pseudo-liberals, and I don't retract the phrase for one moment. I have as much right to think you are a pseudo-liberal as you have to think I am a Red, or as you have to think that I am a menace to the American Civil Liberties Union. I grant you your right of free speech to say what you please about me—as has been said in various publications, in letters, in communications—and I insist that I reserve the right to express my opinion about you. In other words, what I say may not appear to you to be true, but I insist in the A.C.L.U. on my right to say what I believe to be true anywhere and at any place.

In other words, I base my defense on my right to defend myself, my right to free speech, and my right to free press. I may be entirely erroneous in my statements all the way through this article. I don't think I am, but that is beside the point.

138

You don't ask me to prove the truth or falseness of the article; you object to my attitude. I just as strenuously object to your attitude, Mr. Rice. I feel that I don't belong in a Civil Liberties Union where people like you belong, but I would work for your expulsion or for the formulating of a policy in this Union such that people like you wouldn't feel they belong any longer.

I know of at least three members of this Board who I don't think belong on this Board. At least three! I might know more if I thought of it more. But I certainly don't think that Mr. Wise belongs on this Board, or that Morris Ernst belongs on this Board, or that you belong on this Board.

Chairman Holmes: Is there anything further to be said on this charge? Are there any questions to be asked?

Mrs. Bromley: I have just one question. Would you not say, then, Miss Flynn, that the entire majority who passed the Resolution of February 5 do not belong, and then isn't that a reductio ad absurdum?

Miss Flynn: Not altogether. There are different types of people on this Board. There are some people who are on this Board, I think, who are in blissful ignorance of what the A.C.L.U. really stands for. I don't hold it against them, exactly. I think we have made a very poor job of educating them as to what the A.C.L.U. really stands for. I wouldn't say that a person like that shouldn't belong. It would be our duty and responsibility to straighten them out on civil liberties. But I certainly consider that those people on this Board—regardless of majority and minority—who are now abandoning, as I consider it, the fight for labor's rights, and who are making of this Board an open-shop committee—I do not consider that they belong on this Board. That is my opinion, and, by God, I am going to fight for it in the Civil Liberties Union.

Mr. Bingham: I should like to ask a question. In that article, you say, "I don't belong with them anyhow." To whom are you referring?

Miss Flynn: These pseudo-liberals who "take fright." They are the ones I refer to.

Mr. Bingham: That means the majority of the Board?

Miss Flynn: No, I am not sure that the whole majority of the Board takes the position on labor's rights and red-baiting which is particularly objectionable to me.

Mr. Rice: A question of personal privilege! Since I have been personally attacked by Miss Flynn and, by implication, am an advocate of the open shop, I should like to say that never at any time have I taken any open-shop position, and at the present time I am the president of a closed-shop union. I should like to get it on the record.

Miss Flynn: I don't mean that you are not fit to be a member of the A.C.L.U. for that reason, Mr. Rice, but I certainly think you have almost a sort of emotional reaction to Reds—to Communists, in particular—which makes it impossible for you to give impartial consideration to any issue in which they are involved. This isn't a personal attack.

Chairman Holmes: With all due respect, we should not turn the discussion to other members of the Board.

Mr. Hays: Miss Flynn, doesn't this say that you really don't want to associate with us any longer, and that the only reason you didn't resign is that you are making this fight to show us up?

Miss Flynn: Yes, it says that; it says that, certainly. I am not disputing the words.

Mr. Rice: That is the whole basis of my charge.

Miss Flynn: And I would say, Arthur—I will put it in another way: If this resolution which has been passed by the Board of Directors of the Civil Liberties Union is retained by the National Committee and by the membership of the A.C.L.U., then I am afraid I wouldn't belong in the A.C.L.U. But it is because I feel there is a chance to fight you people who have passed this resolution—and I have a right to fight

140

you. Why not? You're fighting me pretty darned hard, aren't you?

Mr. Hays: No question of that.

Miss Flynn: Because I think what you have done is inimical to the interests of the A.C.L.U. You are, to my mind, killing the A.C.L.U.

Mr. Hays: Do you think, Elizabeth, that I would belong on this Board if I went to the public and said all my associates were a bunch of crooks and insincere and that nobody could trust them?

Miss Flynn: I don't say you are a gang of crooks and insincere.

Mr. Hays: If one did say that, if one went to the public prints and said, "All my associates are crooks and an insincere bunch, and I am out to expose them"—if I did say such a thing, do you think I ought to be permitted to serve any longer on that Board, that I am still useful there?

Miss Flynn: I don't think the analogy is exactly fair. What I have discussed here are your points of view and your actions. I haven't called you crooks or called you insincere. I have the most profound respect for Dr. Holmes's sincerity, and I certainly wouldn't call him a crook. But I disagree profoundly with Dr. Holmes's position on labor's rights and employers' rights—in the Ford case and so forth—and I will fight him tooth and nail on that. But there is nothing personal about it.

Mr. Hays: You say here: "In my opinion, the day of the A.C.L.U.'s sincere defense of the civil rights of Communists is over"—suggesting that we aren't sincere.

Miss Flynn: At the time I wrote that, in relation to the Communists, I felt it very strongly; and maybe it is a good thing I wrote this article, because you have come to the defense of Communists much more definitely since this article was written—very much more definitely.

Mr. Hays: That is simply another indication—

Miss Flynn: There has been a most refreshing change in the attitude of the A.C.L.U.

Mr. Hays: Isn't that merely another indication that you don't think we are sincere?

Miss Flynn: Not necessarily. I think you have slipped a long way, Arthur, from the original position of the A.C.L.U., and maybe, by a little strong language, I might have had a little effect to pull you back on the main track. And if I could do that, I am glad I used strong language.

Mr. Finerty: On our record since the article was written, are you willing to publicly repudiate your charges?

Miss Flynn: No, because I am not sure of the motive, Mr. Finerty; I am not sure of the motive.

Mr. Finerty: In other words, you still think we are insincere?

Miss Flynn: I am not sure but what this may be a passing phase, and that you will very soon slip back—not you, Mr. Finerty; I used that word in the wrong sense—but that the A.C.L.U. will soon slip back into the same position again. I don't think you let your right hand know what your left hand is doing here any more, and somebody has to tell you so.

While you expel Miss Flynn as a Communist, you make these fine gestures about the fact that you are going to defend the rights of Communists. Well, then, you suddenly realize you didn't defend any rights of Communists for a long time; so you rush out and defend a few rights of Communists. But I don't know how long you will keep it up. I think this A.C.L.U. Board should face themselves—search their own conscience, as Dr. Holmes says—and find out whether there isn't a lot of lip service about this defense of Communists, and whether you are really going to do it.

If you keep it up, maybe for a year or two, I might take it back. But that you did it just during the period of these partic-

142

ular proceedings against me, and immediately after this article —I am not so sure but that it is expediency, which has been a guiding principle of this Board for too long a period.

Chairman Holmes: Any further questions?

Mr. Spofford: I should like to ask Miss Flynn if she is Irish.

Miss Flynn: You bet I am!

Mr. Lamont: Can we comment on these charges and articles without asking Miss Flynn questions?

Chairman Holmes: I don't see why not.

Mr. Lamont: Later, or now, or when?

Chairman Holmes: After all the evidence is in.

Mr. Isserman: If it is merely argument, it should be reserved. If people want to testify, they should be permitted to do it.

Chairman Holmes: Have you evidence to offer, Mr. Lamont?

Mr. Lamont: I didn't want to prolong discussion on this charge particularly; but I have plenty to say about it.

Chairman Holmes: I think the procedure is to get the evidence in and then have debate.

Mr. Isserman: One point of evidence I think we could add to this record is this: In our Statement of Principles—I don't know just which one; it may be our last Statement of Principles—we have a statement that we don't presume to censor the utterances of our members; and another statement that we don't bind our members to a definition of civil liberties. I think that statement should be added to this record.

Mr. Fraenkel: Those are some of the things that were already in the record in connection with the first charge, and I take it that anything that is in the record can be considered in connection with this charge as well as the first charge.

Mr. Isserman: Is that the understanding?

Chairman Holmes: Quite, quite.

Mr. Hays: Oh, yes.

Mr. Lamont: I have something that I want to try to get in the record here. That is an article by Norman Thomas in the Socialist *Call* of December 16, 1939. Mr. Thomas, in this article, calls a certain group in the Civil Liberties Union hypocrites, calls them insincere, and goes to extremes which made me very, very angry, I must say.

Mr. Thomas was also the first member of the Civil Liberties Union to bring out a public attack on his brother members on this Board. A sub-committee brought in a report that Mr. Thomas's article was highly improper; and it doesn't seem to me that Miss Flynn, or anything Miss Flynn has written, is, on the most extreme interpretation, any worse than Mr. Thomas's article. I think that his article ought to go in the general evidence here.

Mr. Hays: Why not put it in evidence?

Mr. Ernst: Have you the date?

Mr. Lamont: December 16, 1939.

Mr. Isserman: There is another point that the record should contain. On the morning that the consumer report was published by the Dies Committee—it was a Monday, and we had a meeting—Mr. Rice came to the meeting and charged that the Civil Liberties Union Board was Communist-dominated, and also charged that our office was Communist-dominated. An investigation disclosed it was not true as to the office. I think that should be on the record.

Mr. Rice: I never made any such charge, that I recall.

Chairman Holmes: Are there any further statements before we proceed to the third charge? (No response) Mr. Riis, are you ready to present your charge?

Mr. Riis: Yes. I don't know what I am supposed to do. I wrote the letter in question on March 17. I had a witness to the writing of it, I signed and mailed it, and you all read it.

Chairman Holmes: Is that letter here?

144

Mr. Riis: I have a mimeographed copy in my pocket. It is not notarized. (Laughter)

Chairman Holmes: Will you submit that for the record?

Mr. Riis: Yes.

(The document referred to was received in evidence and marked Exhibit No. 4.)

EXHIBIT NO. 4

Letter from Roger W. Riis to Dr. John Haynes Holmes,
March 17, 1940

154 East 74th Street, New York
March 17, 1940

Dr. John Haynes Holmes
10 Park Avenue
New York

Dear Dr. Holmes:

In the matter of Elizabeth Gurley Flynn, the Board of Directors should note her column in the *Daily Worker* of today. I am putting this in writing tonight, so that it will reach the Board tomorrow and be in time to be added to the written charges against Miss Flynn now lodged with the Board.

I take four quotations from the regular column which Miss Flynn signs in the *Daily Worker.*

(1) "The National Committee is a carefully selected list of well known liberals. When they met recently to vote this new policy into effect, they looked like an old men's home out for an afternoon airing."

Calculated to cast ridicule on the National Committee,

this remark reveals Miss Flynn's harsh and contemptuous opinion of that Committee. It is improper for a member of any organization to make public such a statement while still holding membership in that organization.

(2) "Today they (the Board of Directors) . . . are respectable. They . . . play with Mr. Dies for a whitewash. Maybe the price of same was to wash out the red—who knows?"

This is a deliberate and insulting statement that the Board has arranged with Mr. Dies for his approval, provided the Board junks one of its own members. It is ample cause for expelling whatever member of the Board utters it.

(3) "Today they (the Board) are not defending Communists or unions. They are defending 'employers' rights!' "

Miss Flynn here makes a statement she knows is false. She knows the A.C.L.U. is defending Communists and unions, but she chooses to state the opposite to defame the A.C.L.U. I also ask thoughtful attention for the quotation marks which she places around the words "employers' rights," as well as for the exclamation point thereafter. It is to her a comic idea that anyone except Communists or unions have any civil rights. Acting naturally before her own audience, Miss Flynn here throws a brilliant light upon the precise reason why the Board had to adopt the Resolution of February 5th.

(4) "They (the Board) scuttle civil liberties when their security and comfort are menaced. . . . Nice capitalist folk who will assure us, while they sharpen the axe, 'It isn't personal, but I'd rather it would be your head than my check book.' "

The sub-head of this column reads: "American Civil Liberties Union Acts To Cast Out Famed Communist Leader In Order To Save Its Check Book."

One may make every possible allowance for the exaggerations customary to any active politician addressing constitu-

146

ents. One may say that Miss Flynn never intended these words to receive any wider audience than that of the *Daily Worker*. Whatever is urged in exculpation, no one will deny that these words of hers reveal an attitude toward the Board and the Union which disqualify Miss Flynn as a member of the Board. In fact, it is difficult of comprehension why any Director who feels the Board is more devoted to its money than to its principles should insist so stubbornly in maintaining her membership on that Board.

Very truly yours,
(signed) Roger William Riis

•

Mr. Hays: There is something else here to be offered. There is introduced in evidence, on behalf of Miss Flynn, an article written by Norman Thomas, published in the Socialist *Call* on December 16, 1939.

(The document referred to was received in evidence and marked Exhibit No. 5.)

EXHIBIT NO. 5

Article, "Your World and Mine," by Norman Thomas
in Socialist *Call*, December 16, 1939

We must not let our excitement and rage over the European war and the multiplying crimes of Hitler and Stalin blind us to our own unsolved problems. One of these is shamefully illustrated now in my native state of Ohio. While the mayors of Toledo and Cleveland and the governor of the state wrangle, something close to actual starvation has come to thousands of people in a rich and prosperous state.

147

No political leader of that state who cannot do better than its governor has done with this problem deserves consideration on any party's ticket for the presidency as a dark horse or any kind of a horse. The Ohio situation again calls attention to the folly and worse of those who insist that relief should be made exclusively a local or state problem. What is decent in the relief situation in America is due to the interest of the federal government and the improvements which have followed that interest.

One trouble in Ohio, very evident, is the desire of taxpayers to protect themselves by putting constitutional limitations on the kind of taxation and the height of taxation of real estate which is legal. Another trouble seems to be pure politics.

Ward and the A.C.L.U.

It is, by now, a matter of common knowledge that there is a controversy in the American Civil Liberties Union. It centers about Harry F. Ward, long the efficient chairman of the Union, who is also chairman of the American League for Peace and Democracy, an organization which happens to be generally regarded as a Communist innocent front. (Parenthetically I may observe that, under present conditions, the Communist party is likely to drop the league, and that the decent members of the league are likely to break from the party. Already Prof. Ward himself, for the first time, to the best of my knowledge, has publicly criticized an act of Stalin's, at least to the extent of saying that American supplies for war should not go to the Soviet Union. As quoted in *The New York Times* he somewhat spoils the effect of his statement by trying, a little like the Trotskyists, to imply a distinction between Stalin's aggression in Finland and Japan's in China. If anything, Stalin's is the less excusable.)

But to go back to the subject of the American Civil Liberties Union: The controversy really goes much deeper than the issue who should be chairman. It involves the whole concept of the kind of a union which ought to be entrusted with the promotion of civil liberty.

The present board of the American Civil Liberties Union has among its members six or seven Communists or fellow-travelers of various degrees of closeness to the Communist party and the Communist line. In recent years the chairman should be included among them.

Baldwin's Attitude

The situation in America, the need of Communism for protection, and the phase through which the party has passed of professed devotion to democracy, brought it about that no special harm was done to concrete civil liberties by the presence of a minority of members who saw no inconsistency in demanding extreme civil liberty for Communists in America and in defending Stalin for his ruthless denials of them [it].

Roger Baldwin, the Director of the Civil Liberties Union, it is fair to say, has always been outspoken against the brutal betrayal of liberty in Russia. Not so its chairman and some other members.

1934 Incident

The one time when the Communist influence most clearly showed its menace to the A.C.L.U. was back in February, 1934, when the Communists organized the dastardly attack upon the mass meeting in Madison Square Garden in behalf of the gallant Austrian defenders of democracy. At the time of the meeting I was absent on a long speaking trip; a fact that I have never ceased to regret.

I came back in time to be fairly successful in preventing the American Civil Liberties Union from adopting an outrageous whitewash of the whole proceedings, but I was not successful in getting a properly vigorous condemnation of the crime.

Robert Dunn and Mary Van Kleeck actually dissented from the milk and water statement of the majority of the committee in order to defend the right of Communists to break up the meeting when they objected to certain speakers. It is a matter of some ironic amusement that one of the speakers to whom they objected was none other than Mayor La Guardia who, by the way, did not appear, and who a few months later was taken by the Communists to their bosom under its new line.

Communist Position

The episode showed a considerable group in the Civil Liberties Union, including, I am inclined to fear, the chairman, would drop their support of civil liberty the instant Communists were in a position to deny it in the name of some cause dear to them.

The years immediately following 1934 raised no similar issues to the Madison Square Garden outrage. But that Communist fellow travelers had not changed their attitude was again clearly proved when many of them, including the chairman of the Civil Liberties Union, signed, just on the eve of the Stalin-Hitler pact, a completely erroneous defense of Stalin's Russia and a ferocious denunciation of the Committee for Cultural Freedom, and its "initiators," who were Sidney Hook and John Dewey!

Hypocrisy

Now it is quite clear that the American Civil Liberties Union is not and should not be concerned officially with an effort to defend civil liberties in Russia. It is equally clear that men and women of ordinary common sense should not entrust the defense of civil liberties in America to those who condone or fail to denounce, Stalin's purges and his crimes against decency and humanity.

Communists have the right to claim the protection of the American Bill of Rights. They cannot be accepted as honest advocates of them as long as they follow blindly all the changes of policy of the ruthless dictator, Stalin, who proved a thousand times over that he has as little or less conception of civil liberty than the fascist dictators.

Communists belong on the Board of the Civil Liberties Union as much or as little as fascists who also want the protection of the Bill of Rights—until they seize power. To argue the contrary seems to me to be either conscious or subconscious hypocrisy, the product of the sloppiest sort of thinking, or, at the best interpretation, a most fatuous opportunism.

A.C.L.U. Election

To say this is not to argue that the American Civil Liberties Union, or any similar body needs a rigid creed. It can afford, especially in its membership, to include a very considerable variety of opinions about civil liberty. But there are boundaries beyond which it cannot honestly go. There are, for instance, legitimate differences of opinion concerning what constitutes Christian orthodoxy, but no one I ever knew would seriously claim that it was a violation of religious liberty to remove an atheist from a Christian pulpit.

Nor is it a violation of civil liberty to insist that the officers and spokesmen of an organization dedicated to its defense should stand openly for that justice and liberty which Stalin has flouted, to the hurt of the whole world.

I have hoped that the issue to which I refer may be settled and settled right in the American Civil Liberties Union by the time of the annual election, which comes early in February. It is possible that some fellow-travelers may yet return to a genuine belief in liberty. The American League's cautious declaration concerning the Russian attack on Finland may be the beginning of better things.

Reason for Statement

If not, it seems to me necessary for the justification of civil liberties in a troublous time that members and friends of the American Civil Liberties Union, who, as I understand it, have no vote, should exert their influence to see to it that its officers cannot justly be indicted before the bar of public opinion as claiming in behalf of Communists in America those rights which openly or tacitly they support Stalin in denying where he has power. I am hopeful for the result because I greatly prize the work done by the American Civil Liberties Union.

I make this statement because it is a matter of necessity, it seems to me, in the education of public opinion. I also make it as an answer to many questions that have come to me from Socialist comrades concerning my connection with the Union and the things for which it stands.

•

Mr. Riis: The burden of my letter of March 17 is principally in the two last of four numbered paragraphs, where Miss Flynn charges us with defending the rights and civil liberties of any group except labor and Communists—she accuses us of doing that—and, in the last paragraph, she accuses us of having mercenary motives and thinking more of our pocketbooks than of our principles. That is all.

Chairman Holmes: The gist of this charge is the same as the last one—based, however, on a different document.

Mr. Hays: I think that both articles ought to go in evidence in full.

Chairman Holmes: It is so ordered.

Mr. Hays: There is introduced in evidence an article from the *Daily Worker** of March 17, 1940, written by Elizabeth Gurley Flynn, and headed, "I Am Expelled from Civil Liberties!"

(The document referred to was received in evidence and marked Exhibit No. 6.)

EXHIBIT NO. 6

Article by Elizabeth Gurley Flynn
in *Sunday Worker*, March 17, 1940, headed:

I AM EXPELLED FROM CIVIL LIBERTIES!

———

American Civil Liberties Union Acts
to Cast Out Famed Communist Leader
in Order to Save Its Check Book

———

After twenty-three years of association with the group who constitute the American Civil Liberties Union, they now "deem it inappropriate" for me to any longer remain a member of their Board of Directors, and requested me to resign.

*The correct name for the publication here cited is *Sunday Worker.* —Ed.

153

When, unladylike, I refused, they brought charges against me and I am slated for expulsion. Of course, they are all very sorry; I will be a "distinct loss"; there is nothing personal in the matter; they all love me very much; it's such a shame it has to be Elizabeth; her record in fighting for civil liberties is unassailable; it's a most embarrassing procedure and deep regrets are in order!

I feel like an unwanted wife sent to Reno, after all these protestations of affection, except that I don't expect any alimony will be forthcoming. If there should be, I'll give it to the defense of Earl Browder. But I'm not counting on it as Secretary of his Defense Committee!

What crime did I commit that I must be cast into outer darkness? Surely it must be an enormous one to sever such ancient ties. After all, I am a charter member of the A.C.L.U., worked with them during the last war for defense of the wartime political prisoners, then later for Sacco and Vanzetti, the release of Mooney, etc.

My crime is that I am "A MEMBER OF THE COMMUNIST PARTY." *I am to be expelled from the American Civil Liberties Union for my political* VIEWS *and affiliation, a procedure they have continuously protested against if committed by a school, college, or city.*

The funny part of it is, I joined the Communist Party three years ago—not now. I told them at a meeting of the Board of Directors at that time, as a matter of courtesy, not because I considered it obligatory. They all said then it was quite all right, it would make no difference whatsoever. This was in 1937. In 1939 they re-elected me unanimously, knowing I was a Communist, to a three-year term. Two years are still to be served. So there was no deception on my part and no objection on their part. Mr. Roger N. Baldwin, the director, used to boast of their broadness. "Why we even have a Communist on our Board!" and timid old ladies thrilled at his bravery.

Lots of people naturally ask why this sudden change which is a complete reversal of their traditional position? No Communist or supporter of the Soviet Union can now be on the governing body, they decree. The first rebuke to such a surrender of basic civil liberties was the resignation of Dr. Harry F. Ward, Chairman of the organization during twenty years of distinguished service.

I decided to fight, although I have little hope of winning, because, in the contest, the issue will be well aired, and the dues-paying non-voting "members" of the A.C.L.U. may have something to say. The National Committee is a carefully selected list of well known liberals. When they met recently to vote this new policy in effect, they looked like an old men's home out for an afternoon airing! The Board of Directors is even more carefully selected New Yorkers, lawyers, business men, capitalists, ministers, but not a representative of organized labor there. My diagnosis is, they are afraid of labor, especially when it goes to the left. Time was, when the A.C.L.U. was young, they were Anarchists, Socialists, Christian pacifists, trade unionists, I.W.W., Quaker, Irish Republican and Communist! Today, they are no longer heretics, non-conformists, radicals—they are respectable. They cooperate with the Department of Justice; they play with Mr. Dies for a whitewash. Maybe the price of same was to wash out the red—who knows? Today they are not defending Communists or unions. They are defending "employers' rights"!

The trouble is, it's a new world, not 1917. There's a CIO and a Soviet Union. The benign "above the battle" liberals are suddenly aware of the class strug-

155

gle. The Soviet Union let Dr. Holmes down because she didn't act like Gandhi! I have seen shadowed in the eyes of these nice people, so urbane, so courteous, so "tolerant," FEAR OF THE RISING TIDE OF WORKING CLASS POWER. *They chop off my head now in the A.C.L.U. as a gesture of this fear of the Soviet Union and the example she is to the workers of the world.*

They may not know it but they are fighting for their system, capitalism. They scuttle civil liberties when their security and comfort are menaced, and abandon all fights except for their own class. Well, it's better our class enemies come out in their true colors, so working people will not be deceived or misled. If we know them now, we may save ourselves from having our heads actually chopped off in the future by "nice" capitalist folks who will assure us, while they sharpen the axe, "It isn't personal! But I'd rather it would be your head than my check book!"

The change in the A.C.L.U. is a symbol of the profound changes in the world during twenty years. Nobody can straddle the class struggle today. They are capitalist class conscious.

•

Mr. Hays: There is also introduced in evidence an article from the *New Masses* of March 19, 1940, written by Elizabeth Gurley Flynn, and headed, "Why I Won't Resign from the A.C.L.U."

(The document referred to was received in evidence and marked Exhibit No. 7.)

Article by Elizabeth Gurley Flynn
in *New Masses*, March 19, 1940, headed:

WHY I WON'T RESIGN FROM THE A.C.L.U.

———

"Meet the red herring," Elizabeth Gurley Flynn says
in telling the inside story. Penalized for opinion.
Whom will the A.C.L.U. defend?

———

I've been several varieties of a "Red" in my lifetime—Socialist, IWW, Communist—but I never expected to be the proverbial "red herring" in person! As usual, it is to cover an anti-labor, anti-union tendency, but in an unexpected place—the American Civil Liberties Union. This organization, of which I am a charter member, dedicated for twenty years to the defense of the Bill of Rights—free speech, free press, free assemblage, academic freedom, labor's rights, religious freedom, etc.—recently made a complete turnover in policy. A resolution was passed which "deems it inappropriate" that certain persons be on the governing body of the Union (Nazis, fascists, *Communists* and supporters of totalitarian states, including the *Soviet Union*). It was expected that a minority group, labeled most unjustly and inaccurately "a Communist bloc," would withdraw. When this did not happen I was asked to resign from the board of directors, as a member of the Communist Party. This I refuse to do. I do not concede the right of the board to exclude me for my political beliefs and affiliations. The Nazi-fascist stuff in the resolution is just window dressing, as there are no fascists or Nazis on the board. Its inclusion adds insult to injury. Nor do I accept the arbitrary characterization of the Soviet Union. Admiration for the USSR as a workers' country certainly does not label me a totalitarian.

On March 4, Mrs. Dorothy Dunbar Bromley followed my refusal to resign by bringing "charges" against me: "*Elizabeth Gurley Flynn is not entitled to retain directorship on the board on the ground that she is a member of the Communist Party.*" The board, as a committee of the whole, will try me on March 25.* That I am a member of the Communist Party and proud of it is admitted. In fact, when I joined the party three years ago, I announced it to my associates on the board, simply as a matter of courtesy. No one objected then; I was assured it made no difference. In 1939 I was unanimously re-elected to the board for a three-year term, and still have two years to serve. Nothing I have done has changed my status since I was elected.

It is significant that at this same meeting the resignation of Dr. Harry F. Ward from the A.C.L.U. was accepted with formal "regrets" but evident relief, and without even the courtesy of asking him to reconsider, after twenty years of distinguished service as chairman of the Union. His resignation stated his opposition to the recent resolution as "surrendering positions vital to civil liberties." The treatment of Dr. Harry F. Ward by the A.C.L.U. is an indecent and shameful chapter of its secret history: the sidewalk caucus, when a group of directors trooped back to insist that he publicly announce his retirement as chairman *before he testified at the Dies committee hearings* for the American League for Peace and Democracy; their attempts to force him to resign if he remained chairman of the League; their attempt to oust him as "unfit"; their refusal to renominate him as chairman—all topped off with typical bourgeois "politeness," even a cake with candles and a traveling bag as a token of their esteem.

* See footnote, p. 46.—Ed.

The A.C.L.U. was born out of the last war. Present indications are that it is likely to pass out during the present one. Dr. Harry F. Ward is its first casualty; undoubtedly I will be the second; others will follow. I can say in all modesty that there are no two other members whose records surpass ours in defense of the Bill of Rights. Dr. Ward has dealt with his critics with a forbearance they do not deserve. The A.C.L.U. minutes conceal rather than reveal what actually happens. When asked if reports were sent to the active committees around the country, Roger Baldwin, director of the A.C.L.U., replied, "No, they wouldn't know what it was all about." Those who are enrolled as "members of the Union" pay annual dues but are never reported to, or consulted, which wasn't so serious so long as the Union adhered to the basic principles to which they all subscribed. But a radical and fundamental change in policy should be submitted somehow to the membership for discussion and ratification or rejection. Members can voice their protest only by letters to the office. The absence of protest will be construed as agreement. Therefore I am frankly requesting members and active committees of the A.C.L.U. to register their reactions to the resolution; Dr. Ward's resignation; and my forthcoming trial as the only channel of democratic expression from the membership. Please send me copies of your letters.

Dr. Ward said, "The Civil Liberties Union which did this is not the Civil Liberties Union with which I have been proud to work for twenty years." This is literally true. There has been a steady infiltration of new elements who are actually out of sympathy with the traditional position of the A.C.L.U. There are so many wealthy people on the board today that I feel I am to be tried by a "blue ribbon jury." There are lawyers, business men, ministers, but not a single representative of organized labor. Mr. Baldwin, with his customary facility at objections, felt we shouldn't have a CIO representative unless we had one from the AFL, with the result that we have neither. The founders of the A.C.L.U. respected and accepted wide divergence of opinion. I became a member as an IWW and sat with Christian pacifists; with Socialists, anarchists, Irish Republicans, Quakers, trade unionists, liberals, and later Communists.

Mr. Baldwin has stated to the press that persons were never knowingly elected as "Communists" and that William Z. Foster was a respectable AFL organizer when he was elected to the board—a quaint description of a well known Syndicalist who bludgeoned Gompers into organizational campaigns! Foster was a member of the board in 1921 when he joined the CP and was re-elected as such. Anna Rochester was elected as a known member of the Communist Party. Both of them resigned, but not at the request of the board. Mr. Baldwin's "unwritten policy" is just so much sand thrown in the eyes of the public. Not so long ago this breezy fellow-traveler boasted genially of the broadmindedness of the Union. "We even have Communists on our board." All is changed now. Dr. John Haynes Holmes says his conscience will not permit him to sit at the same board with a Communist; Mr. Baldwin says, "Communists have no moral integrity." Well I'll stake mine and any party member's against his any time.

Hitherto the A.C.L.U. has rigidly excluded issues outside of the USA. Now, as Dr. Ward points out, it sets up a test to penalize opinion: "the attitude of persons toward the actions and policies of foreign governments." Its leaders are sore at the Soviet Union—Joseph Stalin didn't consult them on foreign policy! So the A.C.L.U. becomes a victim of the war hysteria it always deplored; sets up a "loyalty oath" such as it has always opposed; attempts to force a minority to accept the views of the majority on issues abroad, or get out. Is this civil liberties? I refused to resign because I will not save the A.C.L.U.'s face or whitewash a betrayal of its basic principles. If the Union is not restored to its original position, its future record is certain to disgrace its traditions. I am fighting to maintain my directorship because I consider the "charges" a violation of every principle the A.C.L.U. has fought for in the past. How can its leaders defend Communists in the right to teach or to hold public office, if they themselves exclude me solely as a Communist? They insist they will defend Communists in the future. I doubt it, if their recent performance is any criterion. There has been a conspicuous inactivity on their part in all our recent cases. Arthur Garfield Hays dashed over to Brooklyn to protest the high bail of the accused Christian Fronters, but never objected for Browder or Wiener. *"The Browder case is not a civil liberties case,"* Mr. Hays informed me. The Mooney case and the Sacco-Vanzetti case were "murder" charges and the Scottsboro case was a "rape" charge to the courts. The A.C.L.U. has been deliberately indifferent to the extradition proceedings against Sam Darcy in Philadelphia and the Schneiderman case in California, although the latter involves cancellation of citizenship for political opinion.

The fishing expedition of federal grand juries in New York and Washington and the disgraceful public attack on Robert Minor, Israel Amter, Alexander Trachtenberg, and others in a publicized letter to the grand jury by former Attorney General Murphy, are unrebuked by the A.C.L.U. The threats against the second class mailing privileges of the *Daily Worker* and *New Masses* go unchallenged. The refusal of the bonding companies to give bail for Communists (which the old A.C.L.U. fought successfully for the IWW) is ignored. No aid was extended to Clarence Hathaway, editor of the *Daily Worker*, in the civil libel suit against him.

In my opinion the day of the A.C.L.U.'s sincere defense of the civil rights of Communists is over. To expect otherwise is to be disappointed. But we must not allow these people to pretend they are doing so by climbing on the bandwagon at the last minute as they did in the Minneapolis WPA cases, which they refused to aid until the trials were over.

The recession of the A.C.L.U. follows the usual red-baiting pattern. It starts with the Communists, but is symptomatic of an anti-labor, anti-union attitude. The test in 1917 was to defend the IWW as labor's furthest outpost; the test in 1940 is to defend the Communist Party. In not defending and in expelling the Communists, the A.C.L.U. exposes its real animus, which is an attack on the rights of labor. That's why I consider myself "a red herring." Mr. Morris Ernst is mightily concerned because John L. Lewis once called the A.C.L.U. "a Communist outfit." He thinks Mr. Lewis will retract this ungracious remark when they throw me out! But I'll be interested to know what the forthright plainspoken chairman of the CIO has to say today of the Union's constant sniping at the Labor Relations Board; of its persistent and unsolicited defense of Henry Ford's "right of free speech" to coerce his employees through leaflet distribution; its attack on the sitdown strike; or Mr. Baldwin's recent insistent demand that the Union make a statement protesting against the invasion of the "civil rights" of the Progressive Miners when they were "forced to join the union" chosen by the majority of the miners, the UMWA; and Norman Thomas' demand that the A.C.L.U. concern itself with expulsion of union members, election disputes, and internal union affairs.

In the A.C.L.U.'s latest statement of principles is a bold declaration for "the right to work" which is identical with that of any open shop, anti-union outfit in the country. Because a pro-labor group fought against these tendencies we were labeled a "Communist bloc." The A.C.L.U. directors have become class conscious. When labor was weak they could afford to be the benign, detached liberals demanding the rights of labor. But labor is strong and powerful today. It needs no wet nurses! These pseudo-liberals take fright at the giant on the horizon which points the possible future everywhere—the Soviet Union. I don't mind being expelled by this kind of people. I don't belong with them anyhow. I'll fight them to expose them, not from a desire to associate with them any longer. Labor can defend its own civil liberties—so can the Communists, without the A.C.L.U.

•

Miss Flynn: I would reiterate, as the basis of my defense, the same basis which I stated in relation to the *New Masses* article—as to my right to defend myself publicly against a public charge, and also my right to express my opinion of this Board and members of this Board as I did.

Now, as to the "mercenary" implication, I think that I was rather justified in that by Mr. Ernst's attempt to have a letter sent out immediately to all those who had lapsed in their membership, calling their attention to this resolution and asking them now to realign themselves with the American Civil Liberties Union. In other words, this resolution was to be made the basis for a financial appeal to those who would approve of the elimination of Communists from the Board.

His motion wasn't carried—I don't know why, it wasn't seconded, or for some reason it wasn't carried—but the idea was carried forth in a letter which went out from the office on April 19, signed by Mr. Huebsch as Chairman of the Membership Advisory Committee, and sent to us as the Board members.

In that letter, he said:

"Dear Fellow Director: This seems the ideal time to promote our old plan to increase the membership of the Union.

The organization has never been more highly regarded by the press and public than now, and a determined effort will bring us declared adherents in larger numbers and contributions in larger volume than at any period in our twenty years."

It seems to me that that is the method that has so often characterized our office. When a thing was voted down here by the Board, they found another way to do the same job. And here it is in this letter of April 19.

I submit that that justifies me in saying there were mercenary motives. I don't mean that in relation to individual members of the Board, but in relation to—well, may I say in relation to the office and to those who proposed there should be capitalization of our anti-Communist stand.

Mr. Hays: Will you offer that in evidence?

Miss Flynn: Yes, I will offer this letter in evidence.

Mr. Huebsch: May I interject here that we haven't by any means received enough money in response to this letter.

Mr. Hays: May we have this letter marked?

Miss Flynn: A letter to the Board of Directors, April 19, 1940, signed by B. W. Huebsch as Chairman of the Membership Advisory Committee.

(The letter referred to was received in evidence and marked Exhibit No. 8.)

Letter from B. W. Huebsch to the Directors of the A.C.L.U., April 19, 1940

American Civil Liberties Union
31 Union Square West
New York City

April 19, 1940

Dear Fellow Director:

This seems the ideal time to promote our old plan to increase the membership of the Union. The organization has never been more highly regarded by the press and public than now, and a determined effort will bring us declared adherents in larger numbers and contributions in larger volume than at any period in our twenty years.

Pursuant to the Board's action of some months ago our Committee secured the assistance of Edgar Sherman of Raymond Rich Associates, and a plan for quick action before the season is too far advanced is ripe for execution.

In order to carry out the plan we need to have $3000 for printing, postage, purchase of lists of names, and incidental expenses. We are reasonably sure of favorable returns not only in the matter of money but in memberships which will be a source of future income.

All of the above was stated at last Monday's meeting, but I am sending this letter so that every Director may be informed and in order to secure quick and effective action. The Board approved our Committee's plans for the membership drive and a proposal to secure the needed money through voluntary effort of the members of the Board. Thus we need contributions which may be outright gifts or in the nature of underwriting, on an average of $100 for each Board member. Three or four members of the Board have already volunteered to be responsible for $100 each, and my purpose in writing to you is to request that you will consider our immediate need and let me know whether and to what extent we may count on you.

Yours sincerely,
B. W. Huebsch, Chairman,
Membership Advisory Committee

•

Miss Flynn: One more remark: It struck me as rather humorous that when I made an implication in an article that members of this Board were class conscious, they immediately demonstrated it by the ferociousness with which they proceeded to demand my expulsion from the Union.

I still insist that if I want to say that members of this Board are class conscious, I have a right to say so. Of course, from a working class standpoint, that is not an insult; but apparently, in these unhappy days, it is an insult to say that a member of the capitalist class is class conscious.

I won't take up any more of your time. My basis is my right to free speech and to defend myself.

Mr. Dunn: I want to ask one question. Might you not also have been influenced in this implication of a mercenary attitude by the report made here one day—I believe by Mrs. Bromley herself—to the effect that the letters of approval of the resolution which had come in had been accompanied by sizable checks, while those coming in the way of protest had not been so accompanied? Perhaps that might have been in your mind, too.

Miss Flynn: It may have been. A lot of water has run under the bridge since then, and, I tell you frankly, I don't know that I could write as good an article for the *New Masses* or the *Sunday Worker* today as I was able to write then. All the things that were right at my finger-tips then I can't refer to now. But I did hear Mrs. Bromley make that report.

Mr. Hays: I have just one question—whether you put in this headline, or that was put in by the editor: "American Civil Liberties Union Acts to Cast Out Famed Communist Leader in Order to Save Its Check Book."

Miss Flynn: No, I didn't do that.

Mr. Ernst: My name has been mentioned. I made no answer to any of the comments; they were just too silly. But I don't want this record to close without stating—and I could ask Elizabeth a question, but I will state it—that I look with great disapproval on the attacks on Roger Baldwin and the Chairman of this Board in the statement read by Elizabeth Gurley Flynn. Period!

Mr. Greene: This last charge has been advanced by Mr. Riis. Evidently, he desires to lay down some strictures on the scope of speech permissible to a member of this Board.

I have here a copy of a letter—also not notarized—written by Mr. Riis in September, 1938, to Mr. Roger Baldwin. It was written at a juncture of our history when we were debating the Ford case, and Mr. Riis was very impatient about the Board's action on the Ford case, or its failure to act as quickly as he wanted it to act. So he wrote a letter.

He said: "I am getting close to the last point of exasperation on this whole situation. During the summer I wrote Mr. Britchey that sometime during the fall I would like to have the Board reveal its general attitude toward the desirability of permitting a Federal body to delimit the borders of free speech. I have this morning a copy of a letter Dr. Holmes sent you yesterday and thoroughly agree with him." O.K.

"As a personal matter it's putting me in a dreadful spot with regard to the *Reader's Digest* article"—which he was planning to write.

"Honest reporting, to which I have some sentimental devotion, compels me to touch on this question and to reveal what I consider is the iniquity of the Civil Liberties Union in this situation. Devotion to the major work the Union is doing induces me to slur the thing over. In the long run, however, I think I shall sleep better if I do an honest job of reporting, and the net result will be pretty bad for the Union.

"If you wish to you can regard this as blackmail. I would gladly resort to blackmail if I thought it would straighten out this preposterous situation on the Civil Liberties Board.

"Sincerely, R. W. Riis."

Mr. Hays: Did that appear in the press?

Mr. Greene: No, it did not.

Mr. Ernst: Was the letter ever made public?

Mr. Riis: Relatively public, yes. The letter is quite correct.

Mr. Ernst: Did you send the letter to the press?

Mr. Riis: No; to Roger. I should like to ask Mr. Baldwin if he knows me well enough to have interpreted the remark about blackmail as Mr. Greene did, who doesn't know me so well.

Mr. Baldwin: No, the references were humorous—to me.

Mr. Greene: Were the references to "iniquity" also humorous?

Mr. Riis: Yes, sir.

Mr. Hays: There is offered in evidence a letter of September 28, 1938, from Mr. R. W. Riis to Mr. Roger Baldwin.

(The letter referred to was received in evidence and marked Exhibit No. 9.)*

Mrs. Bromley: In this connection, I should like to know —I ought to remember, but I don't—what the upshot was of the *Reader's Digest* article. Did Mr. Riis in print make any sweeping condemnation of the Board's action?

Mr. Riis: No, I presented both sides, I think, with a good

---

* I was unable to locate Exhibit No. 9, but virtually the full text of the letter is printed on pp. 167-68.—Ed.

deal more fairness than I should have—I mean the side with which I disagreed. I heard no complaint from any of the members who are now complaining.

Mr. Greene: It should be borne in mind that the Board eventually took substantially the actions Mr. Riis wanted them to.

Mr. Lamont: Could I ask you a question, Mr. Chairman?

Chairman Holmes: Certainly.

Mr. Lamont: Did you write the letter Miss Flynn refers to—in connection with Miss Luscomb—on February 15? I will just take it out of her brief: "If you knew what we have been through in recent months, how our work has been delayed, made of non-effect, sabotaged, by members of our Board who have no belief in civil liberties except from the standpoint of their own particular interests, you would sympathize with and support the action we have taken."

Chairman Holmes: I either wrote that or stated it at the Boston meeting—I don't know which.

Mr. Lamont: It would imply that some members of this Board were rather insincere in their support of civil liberties, I should say.

Chairman Holmes: I wouldn't say "insincere"; I would say they don't know anything about it.

Mr. Lamont: "Have no belief in civil liberties except from the standpoint of their own particular interests."

Chairman Holmes: Exactly.

*Mr. Lamont: When did this come to your attention?

Chairman Holmes: Miss Luscomb sent me a copy.

Mr. Lamont: Do you know how long ago?

Chairman Holmes: Within the last few weeks.

Mr. Lamont: After the charges were made?

---

* The text throughout follows the original transcript faithfully. It is obvious, however, that the transcript here contains stenographic errors. In the six lines following the asterisk the statements attributed to Mr. Lamont were made by Chairman Holmes, and vice versa.—Ed.

Chairman Holmes: Oh, yes, yes—just recently.

Mr. Lamont: I bring this up, Mr. Chairman, simply to comment that I think this is an outrageous and untrue statement, in the first place—

Mr. Finerty: A point of order!

Chairman Holmes: No points of order.

Mr. Finerty: There is a point of order. You can't protect yourself, and you are entitled to be protected against attacks having nothing to do with this matter.

Mr. Lamont: Let me say what it has to do with it.

Chairman Holmes: Proceed, Mr. Lamont.

Mr. Lamont: We have been in a first-class political fight here for over a year. The battle has waged back and forth, and has become very bitter whenever this issue comes up. The Board functions very well when it doesn't come up. Even Elmer Rice knows what civil liberties are about when he isn't thinking about Stalin. The fact is that Miss Flynn's articles in the *New Masses* and the *Daily Worker* and all the rest of this bickering are a reply—and, I think, a very fully justified kind of reply—to the sort of thing that has been going on in the Civil Liberties Union from the other side, starting away back and going on with Mr. Thomas's article in the Socialist *Call*, and coming very much up to date with statements that you and Mr. Baldwin and others have made to our local committees and to other persons.

I think that Miss Flynn's articles have to be considered in light of this fact that we have been in a very bitter battle, and that some people here—in fact, most people here—have gotten rather excited.

Mr. Seymour: May I ask Mr. Lamont a question?

Mr. Lamont: Absolutely.

Mr. Seymour: Would you agree that, during the last year, aspects of this controversy have seriously affected the ability of the Board to deal with its week-to-week work on other civil liberty matters?

Mr. Lamont: Will you let me give you a full answer on that?

Mr. Seymour: Surely.

Mr. Lamont: I should say yes, that since we passed the resolution of March 6, 1939, saying that the Union would make no statement in opposition to any form of government, Mr. Morris Ernst and a group associated with him on this Board have constantly brought up this Communist issue—week after week, and month after month. It has embittered our work and made it almost impossible at times. But, in every instance, Mr. Ernst and that group have been the aggressors—

Mr. Rice: Like Finland.

Mr. Lamont: No member of this so-called minority—certainly not Miss Flynn—has taken any part in trying to get anybody thrown out, or in passing any purge resolutions, or anything of the sort. That issue—that Communist issue—whenever it has come up, has aroused necessarily such bitter feeling on both sides of the Board that it has interfered with our work.

The idea here that there has been plotting and so forth by members of the Board is not borne out by any evidence. I challenge you or anybody else on the Board to find one single vote or one single decision that this Board has taken where Miss Flynn or anybody else has sabotaged, filibustered, or deliberately tried to delay the work of the Board for their particular interests or the interests of some particular group.

Mr. Seymour: I am not trying to defend that statement, but there is no doubt at all that, in the last year, the existence of this controversy in the Board has seriously interfered with its efficiency and functioning as a Board.

Mr. Lamont: There is no doubt at all.

Mr. Hays: I think the record ought to show that, of all the people of the so-called "left" group, Elizabeth Flynn has done less to impede the progress of work; she hasn't made long talks—

Mr. Fraenkel: May I ask Mr. Hays—

Mr. Hays: She hasn't interrupted proceedings—

Mr. Seymour: I am just asking a general question.

Mr. Hays: If there has been that, it certainly hasn't been by Miss Flynn.

Mr. Fraenkel: May I ask Mr. Hays a question?

Mr. Hays: Yes.

Mr. Fraenkel: As I understood Mr. Lamont's remarks, they were to the effect that the work of the Board had been impeded by the revival, from time to time—and, latterly, consistently—of an issue which many of us thought has [had] been settled by the vote taken in March of 1939. Would you agree with that?

Mr. Hays: Yes.

Mr. Fraenkel: Now, that issue was not revived by any-one of the left-wing group, was it?

Mr. Hays: No.

Chairman Holmes: We are proceeding now, evidently, to a discussion of the general situation. If there are no further questions or observations about the third charge, the Chairman will now say that we have the question before us as to the method of action upon these three charges. Mr. Bingham, are you talking on that?

Mr. Bingham: I was going to ask permission to introduce a resolution dealing with all three charges.

Chairman Holmes: You don't need any permission.

Mr. Hays: May I ask whether Miss Flynn should be present during our discussion? I wonder whether we can't talk more frankly about these charges if Miss Flynn isn't here. I don't think she should be here while we discuss the charges and vote on them.

Chairman Holmes: Miss Flynn, it has been suggested that it would be proper for you to retire. Is there anything more for you to say?

Miss Flynn: It depends on what you say.

Mr. Finerty: Is there any comfortable place to which she can retire?

Mr. Isserman: Yes, out here—

Chairman Holmes: Very good. Miss Flynn, we will ask you to retire.

(Miss Flynn left the room.)

(There was off-the-record discussion.)

Chairman Holmes: The motions that have been made during the discussion that has taken place so far, and the objections, and so forth, may be stated for the record.

Mr. Fraenkel: I made a motion to dismiss the first charge on the ground that the charge in itself was insufficient to justify expulsion, because the fact that Miss Flynn was a member of the Communist Party was known at the time of her election in 1939, and that nothing brought out at this hearing in connection with the first charge justifies expulsion. On motion of Mr. Nunn, my motion was tabled for the time being.

Then Mr. Hays moved that a straw ballot be taken as to the guilt or innocence of Miss Flynn on each of the three charges, sustaining or not sustaining each of the three charges; and Mr. Isserman protested against that method of procedure on the ground—

Mr. Isserman: —that the ballot was improper, and on the ground that the motion to dismiss had not been disposed of. Also, at the time that Mr. Fraenkel made his motion to dismiss, I noted my own request, previously made, to supplement Mr. Fraenkel's motion by a motion of my own; and that request was carried over with the motion to table.

Also, we objected to a consideration of the three charges on one ballot and by one vote, and urged that each charge be voted on separately.

Mr. Fraenkel: I concurred in that objection, and Mr. Isserman and I refrained from taking any part in the straw ballot because we considered it improper and irregular.

Mr. Hays: The motion I made was that a straw ballot be

taken so that we could all express our views; that no record be made of the vote, but that [it] merely be taken so that we could get an idea about how we all felt about this proposition. That motion was carried, and the Chairman stated that subsequently Mr. Fraenkel's motion would be put and properly argued—Mr. Fraenkel's and Mr. Isserman's.

Mr. Fraenkel: I want to add to my objection to the taking of a straw ballot the point that until there had been argument and discussion on the merits of the charges, I thought it was improper to take any kind of ballot.

Chairman Holmes: The result of the straw ballot was announced.

(There was further off-the-record discussion.)

Mr. Fraenkel: I move that Charge Number 1 be dismissed.

Mr. Hays: A question of information! Does that mean that the charge that Elizabeth was a Communist was not sustained, or that that is not a ground for expelling a member?

Mr. Fraenkel: The fact that she is a Communist has never been disputed. My motion is that the charge is insufficient as a charge against a Director both because of the facts stated in the original charge and on the basis of the evidence here produced—insufficient to justify any disciplinary action whatever under our by-laws.

Mr. Greene: I second it.

Mr. Isserman: I join in that motion without amplifying it. I will reserve my amplification for argument later.

(Mr. Fraenkel presented an argument in favor of his motion, following which there was further off-the-record discussion.)

Mr. Isserman: I move to dismiss the charge against Miss Flynn—Charge Number 1—on the ground that we are a membership corporation and bound by the laws of the State of New York; that our by-laws set up qualifications for mem-

174

bership; that the resolution in question is no qualification for membership; that the resolution in question is too vague to set up any standard by means of which a judgment can be arrived at; that the resolution is in conflict with existing resolutions of the Civil Liberties Union—namely, the one which reads that we bind our members to no definition of civil liberties; and that the resolution is contra to the objects of the Civil Liberties Union.

(There was further off-the-record discussion.)

Mr. Fraenkel: I withdraw my motion, for the time being, so Mr. Isserman's motion stands and can be voted on.

Chairman Holmes: Will Mr. Isserman state his motion?

Mr. Isserman: My motion goes really to the legal sufficiency of this procedure and is directed to the status of this case before any evidence was introduced.

Chairman Holmes: Will you repeat your motion?

Mr. Isserman: It is a motion to dismiss on the grounds that I previously outlined; and I should like to ask the stenographer to repeat them, if that is necessary.

Chairman Holmes: I don't think it is necessary to repeat them.

Mr. Isserman: What I am saying, in essence, is this: Considering our by-laws, considering our charter, considering the laws under which we operate—we are a membership corporation—considering this resolution, and considering the charges Mrs. Bromley filed, we should have thrown the whole thing out of the window; and my motion is that we throw it out of the window.

(There was further off-the-record discussion.)

Mr. Nunn: I make a substitute motion that the charge brought by Mrs. Bromley be sustained. I would be willing to withdraw that if Mr. Isserman would phrase his motion, "that the charge brought by Mrs. Bromley be dismissed"; but, since he won't—

Mr. Ernst: I second the motion.

(Mr. Isserman made a point of order that Mr. Nunn's substitute motion was out of order. He was overruled by the Chair. Mr. Isserman appealed from the ruling of the Chair, a vote was taken, and the ruling of the Chair was sustained.)

(Mr. Nunn's motion to sustain the first charge was put to a vote. There were 9 votes in favor of the motion and 9 opposed, with Dr. Holmes, Mr. Bingham and Mr. Frank not voting. Thereupon Dr. Holmes voted affirmatively, making the vote 10 in favor and 9 opposed. Voting in favor of the motion, in addition to Dr. Holmes, were: Mrs. Bromley, Mr. Carmer, Mr. Ernst, Mr. Huebsch, Miss Lasker, Mr. Nunn, Mr. Rice, Mr. Riis and Mr. Seymour. Voting against the motion were: Mr. Dunn, Mr. Finerty, Mr. Fraenkel, Mr. Greene, Mr. Hays, Mr. Isserman, Miss Kenyon, Mr. Lamont and Mr. Spofford.)

Mr. Hays: In view of the fact that our names have been taken, I want to put this on the record—that I believe that the fact that a person is a member of the Communist Party is not necessarily a reason for firing the person from the Board. If I believe that that person, as an individual, believes in civil liberties, is a good fighter for civil liberties, is sincere in it; and that, if the issue arises between the Communist Party and the Civil Liberties Union, then she will take her position; and if I believe in that person's sincerity, I won't vote to expel her because she is a member of the Communist Party.

But I am not prepared to take the position that Mr. Isserman is prepared to take—that membership in the Communist Party ipso facto is not a reason for dismissal—because it may well be reason for dismissal with a great many individuals.

Mr. Finerty: My reason for voting against the first charge is that, in voting for the resolution, I considered it purely prospective; and I think it would be the negation of civil liberties in the Civil Liberties Union to make a retroactive

176

application of the resolution, inasmuch as, at the time Miss Flynn accepted membership in the Communist Party, it was known to the Civil Liberties Union, and after she became a Communist she was re-elected to the Board.

I want to make quite clear that I do consider membership in the Communist Party as per se disqualifying one for membership otherwise in the Civil Liberties Union.

Mr. Isserman: I support everything Mr. Hays said, except the last thing. In other words, I go one step further than he; and that is that at the time this resolution was passed, there was nothing demonstrated which would indicate that membership in the Communist Party was inconsistent with membership on the Board of the Civil Liberties Union and service on behalf of civil liberties in the United States.

Mr. Frank: I want to say just one thing. I don't take a position one way or the other as to membership in the Communist Party. I say that it depends on the circumstances of each particular situation. That is why I didn't vote—because I didn't think that the circumstances of this case justified any action.

Mr. Seymour: I move that the motions to dismiss, which are still pending, be now denied in view of the action just taken.

Mr. Ernst: I second it.

Mr. Isserman: I object to that on the ground that the motion to dismiss is not pending. There was a substitute motion adopted, and the present motion is out of order. You have precluded yourselves from voting on that motion.

Chairman Holmes: All right.

(There was further off-the-record discussion.)

Chairman Holmes: Do I hear a motion for Charge Number 2? Mr. Rice made that charge.

Mr. Rice: I move the charge be sustained.

Mr. Huebsch: I second it.

(There was discussion of the motion. The motion was then put to a vote and was carried by a vote of 12 to 8, with Dr. Holmes not voting. Those voting in favor of the motion were: Mrs. Bromley, Mr. Carmer, Mr. Ernst, Mr. Finerty, Mr. Frank, Mr. Hays, Mr. Huebsch, Miss Lasker, Mr. Nunn, Mr. Rice, Mr. Riis and Mr. Seymour. Those voting against the motion were: Mr. Bingham, Mr. Dunn, Mr. Fraenkel, Mr. Greene, Mr. Isserman, Miss Kenyon, Mr. Lamont and Mr. Spofford.)

Chairman Holmes: We will now take up Charge Number 3. Do you want to make a motion, Mr. Riis?

Mr. Riis: Yes, the surprising motion that the charge be sustained.

Mr. Finerty: I second it.

Mr. Isserman: The only thing I want to say is to repeat the argument against this charge that I made against the previous one.

(The motion was put to a vote and carried by a vote of 12 to 8, with Dr. Holmes not voting. Those voting in favor of the motion were: Mrs. Bromley, Mr. Carmer, Mr. Ernst, Mr. Finerty, Mr. Frank, Mr. Hays, Mr. Huebsch, Miss Lasker, Mr. Nunn, Mr. Rice, Mr. Riis and Mr. Seymour. Those voting against the motion were: Mr. Bingham, Mr. Dunn, Mr. Fraenkel, Mr. Greene, Mr. Isserman, Miss Kenyon, Mr. Lamont and Mr. Spofford.)

Mr. Fraenkel: I should like to record a brief statement of my reason for my vote on this and the last motion. While I think that the articles in question were unfortunate in their phrasing, and, in some respects, indefensible, I think that under the circumstances—particularly in light of the action taken by the Board in connection with Norman Thomas's article—they could have been passed over in the same way, and should not have formed the basis of any charges.

Chairman Holmes: The charges have now been sustained and there remains one item of business. That is what you call "punishment"—I don't like to call it punishment—let us say, "what to do about it."

Mr. Rice: If a motion is in order, I move that Miss Flynn be removed from the Board.

Mr. Riis: I second it.

(There was discussion on the motion.)

Mr. Fraenkel: I move to table the motion before us.

(There was further off-the-record discussion.)

Mr. Fraenkel: I move that any further action be postponed for a time.

Chairman Holmes: That wouldn't be in order, with a motion before the house.

Mr. Fraenkel: My motion is a motion to table, to take it up at a later date—at a date to be fixed later.

Mr. Seymour: I second that.

(The motion to table was put to a vote and defeated.)

(Mr. Rice's motion that Miss Flynn be removed from the Board was put to a vote and was carried by a vote of 11 to 8, with Dr. Holmes not voting. Voting in favor of the motion were: Mrs. Bromley, Mr. Carmer, Mr. Ernst, Mr. Finerty, Mr. Huebsch, Miss Lasker, Mr. Nunn, Mr. Rice, Mr. Riis, Mr. Seymour and Mr. Spofford. Voting against the motion were: Mr. Bingham, Mr. Dunn, Mr. Fraenkel, Mr. Greene, Mr. Hays, Mr. Isserman, Miss Kenyon and Mr. Lamont. Mr. Frank had left the meeting before the vote was taken.)

Mr. Spofford: I want it recorded that I voted for this motion so that it would go to the National Committee, since that is the only way it could get to the National Committee.

Mr. Rice: I move that the absent members be polled; that they be informed of the vote on the various charges—with the names of the members, if they desire it, voting on either side; that the vote on this final question be also reported to them; and that their votes be—I will withdraw the motion.

(Whereupon, at 2:20 A.M., the meeting adjourned.)

179

PART III

APPENDICES

WHY WE DEFEND FREE SPEECH FOR NAZIS, FASCISTS AND COMMUNISTS

An answer to critics who would deny liberty to
those they characterize as enemies of democracy

By the Board of Directors of the
American Civil Liberties Union

April, 1939

Since the spread of totalitarian governments in Europe, and the fear in the United States for the fate of democracy, the Civil Liberties Union has been increasingly urged both by friends and critics to take a position denying freedom of speech to the movements those persons characterize as anti-democratic. They have also urged that we declare ourselves in opposition to all anti-democratic theories and forms of government, even if we continue to defend the rights of their advocates.

The attitude of these friends and critics is quite understandable, though it is wholly foreign to the aims and work of the Civil Liberties Union.

The Union does not engage in political controversy.

It takes no position on any political or economic issue or system.

It defends without favoritism the rights of all-comers, whatever their political or economic views.

It is wholly unconcerned with movements abroad or with foreign governments.

An organization to defend civil liberties naturally stands in direct opposition to any movement which rejects the principles contained in the Bill of Rights. *But this opposition is expressed at the point of action contrary to the Bill of Rights, not in relation to theories.* It is the task of other organizations to engage in political controversy in defense of democracy. It is our task to help preserve democracy by opposing all violations of the Bill of Rights from any source whatever.

It is in this spirit that we defend even the rights of those who might, if they came to power, suppress civil liberty. We certainly cannot abandon the principles of the Bill of Rights, which requires defense of everybody's rights without distinction, just because of the fear that thus some anti-democratic force will triumph. Such a fear implies distrust of democracy.

The defenders of civil liberty cannot tolerate the suppression of any propaganda. We support only the suppression of *acts* in violation of civil liberty, or actual preparation for the use of force. Beyond that we cannot go and remain faithful to our purposes. Nor is it our function to indulge in characterizing movements as democratic or anti-democratic.

The best way to combat propaganda directed against the principles of the Bill of Rights is in the open where it can be fought by counter-propaganda, protest demonstrations, picketing —and all the devices of attack which do not involve denying the right to meet and speak. Defenders of civil liberty cannot yield to government the right to discriminate between those who may enjoy the protection of the Bill of Rights and those who may not.

To those who advocate *suppressing propaganda they hate*, we reply that they can draw no consistent line. What one would suppress, another would not. The only clear place to draw a line is between words on the one hand and acts or attempted acts, or incitements to specific unlawful acts on the other. For scurrilous statements against individuals or organizations which do not amount to incitements, the libel laws are adequate.

It is clear that free speech as a practical tactic as well as an abstract principle, demands defense of the rights of *all* who are attacked in order to maintain the rights of *any*. It was for precisely that reason that two of our attorneys, both Jews, urged on the Mayor of New York the use of city property for a meeting of the persecutors of Jews, the Nazis; and that our general counsel, a Jew, aided the attorney for the Friends of New Germany (Nazi) in court proceedings to break down a lawless prohibition of their meetings in New Jersey. Just so, some years ago, the Union protested denial of rights to the Ku Klux Klan by the Catholic mayor of Boston on the ground that if he could stop the Klan, he could lawlessly stop others he disliked—the Communists, birth control advocates, and pacifists. And he did. Our protest began where his lawless suppression began.

To those who urge *suppression of meetings that may incite riot or violence,* the complete answer is that nobody can tell in advance what meetings may do so. Where there is reasonable ground for apprehension, the police can ordinarily prevent disorder without suppressing the meeting.

To those who would *suppress meetings where race or religious prejudice is likely to be stirred up,* the answer is simple— that there is no general agreement on what constitutes race or religious prejudice. Once the bars are so let down, the field is open for all-comers to charge such prejudice against any group— Catholics, Jehovah's Witnesses, atheists—even against Jews attacking the Nazis. On that ground the Union has opposed in state legislatures the anti-Nazi bills introduced that propose to punish propaganda which, in the opinion of some court might "stir up race or religious hatred" or "domestic strife." No laws can be written to outlaw Nazi propaganda without striking at freedom of speech in general.

Further we point out the inevitable effect of making martyrs by persecution. To persecute any movements so as to drive them underground would attract hundreds of sympathizers who would otherwise be indifferent. The issue would become that of their liberties, not their purposes.

But against interference by one group with the rights of any other group, the Union will fight. Against preparations for the use of force, the Union is urging the enactment of laws to prohibit military drill or arms in the hands of private organizations. In the Klan's hey-day the Union championed laws unmasking them in public parades, while supporting their right to meet, in hoods and gowns, on private property. Masking identity in public parades for purposes of intimidation is quite different from indulging in secret rites, masked where no outsiders need look on.

We urge upon our friends and critics alike a careful consideration of the policy of the Union set forth here. It is the same policy to which every public official is pledged under our constitutional guarantees. No other policy will preserve democratic institutions. Those who would except from the protection of the Bill of Rights the forces they fear as anti-democratic should consider the lessons of history. When the rights of *any* are sacrificed, the rights of *none* are safe.

"A STATEMENT TO MEMBERS AND FRIENDS OF THE AMERICAN CIVIL LIBERTIES UNION," RELEASED TO THE PRESS BY THE A.C.L.U. ON FEBRUARY 5, 1940

The Board of Directors and the National Committee of the American Civil Liberties Union feel an obligation to state to members and friends the reasons which prompt the adoption of a resolution which appears to set up a test of opinion. The resolution does not, however, change the fundamental policy of the Union over the twenty years of its existence. The Union has never originally elected to its Board of Directors nor its National Committee persons whose support of civil liberties for everybody without distinction appeared to be qualified.

The Union has always recognized that membership in the Communist Party, as in certain other groups, involves a conception of civil liberties quite different from that of the Union. No member of the Communist Party was therefore ever elected or appointed to any position of responsibility in the Union. Two members of the National Committee, however, joined the Communist Party some years after their election, and the Board did not think it necessary to disassociate them on the ground of their political opinions. One of them, William Z. Foster, elected when he was an organizer for the A. F. of L. in 1920, served some years and resigned in disagreement on a matter of policy. The other, Elizabeth Gurley Flynn, one of the original incorporators of the Union, did not join the Communist Party until fifteen years later. She has since served on the Board of Directors and is the only member of the Communist Party on the Board.

The occasion for raising this issue at this time is the increasing tension which has resulted everywhere from the direction of the Communist international movement since the Soviet-Nazi pact. The abandonment of the struggle against Fascism and the other changes in Communist policy have raised sharp issues which were reflected in the attitudes of members of our Board of Directors.

Nobody suggests that any person should be excluded from membership in the Union, nor that the Union should be any less zealous in the defense of Communists' rights. The sole issue raised is one of propriety affecting the governing committees in terms of a consistent attitude in support of the principle of civil liberties.

The present resolution merely states what has been always the unwritten policy of the Union in elections or appointments. Its sole effect will be to apply that policy to present membership.

OPEN LETTER TO THE A.C.L.U. FROM
SEVENTEEN LIBERALS, MARCH 18, 1940

We appeal publicly to the American Civil Liberties Union to rescind its recent purge resolution as unworthy of its traditions and incompatible with its principles.

In the past, loyalty to the Bill of Rights in America has been the sole requirement imposed by the Civil Liberties Union on its members and its officers, and this should continue as always to be its only criterion. In the two decades of its existence the Union has concentrated its energies on one job alone—the defense of civil liberties at home. It has steadfastly refused to go beyond that task. It has resisted, as inconsistent with its fundamental aims, any attempt to involve it in questions concerning civil liberties abroad or forms of government. As a result, it has had the broadest kind of support from persons holding all sorts of divergent political views and has kept its ranks undivided by questions with no direct bearing on its purposes. During those twenty years its enemies would have been happy at any time to divert the energies of the Union from defense of civil rights at home to endless debate on events abroad. They seem to have succeeded at last.

We believe that by the purge resolution the American Civil Liberties Union encourages the very tendencies it was intended to fight. It sets an example less liberal organizations will not be slow to imitate. It places the prestige of our foremost defender of civil liberties behind the idea that Communists or Communist sympathizers or that infinitely extensible category of "fellow-travelers" are properly to be barred from certain types of offices and treated as less than first-class citizens.

The resolution "regards it as inappropriate" for any person to serve on the governing committees or the staff of the Civil Liberties Union "who is a member of any political organization which supports totalitarian dictatorship in any country, or who by his public declarations and connections indicates his support of such a principle." This category, according to the resolution, includes not only Communist, Nazi or Fascist parties but "native organizations with obvious anti-democratic objectives or practices, such as the Ku Klux Klan, the Silver Shirts, Christian Front and others."

These standards are extremely loose and broad. When the Civil Liberties Union opposed the original resolution for the Dies Committee investigation, it objected properly that the terms of that resolution were "dangerously vague." But the categories now established by the Civil Liberties Union itself are vague enough to satisfy Dies himself and far more dangerous because they come from an organization whose function is to defend civil liberties.

The real effect of this resolution is to give the Union an opportunity to purge itself of Communists and those suspected of any sympathy with Communists. The reference to Nazis and Ku Kluxers and Silver Shirts can hardly be taken seriously since, unlike the Communists, they have never fought for civil liberties in this country. They do not believe in civil liberty here or anywhere else, now or at any other time.

They would no more join the Civil Liberties Union than they would the B'nai B'rith or the National Association for the Advancement of Colored People. The Union, by "barring" them from office, has taken a less than momentous step.

Furthermore, this resolution, like the type of "loyalty" legislation the Union has fought so often, does not confine itself to members of the Communist Party. It applies to all those who support "totalitarian dictatorship" in any country. What is a totalitarian dictatorship? Is war-time France, with its concentration camps, and its rigid controls of fundamental rights, democratic or totalitarian? And is not the American Civil Liberties Union necessarily ruling out those faithful Catholics who, following the policy laid down by their Church, approve the Fascist regimes in Spain and Italy?

The word "support" is never too clear, but what is one to say of the reference to any person who "by his public declarations *and connections indicates* his support of such a principle"? What is meant by "connections" and what are sufficient "indications"? What are "native organizations with obvious anti-democratic objectives or practices"? What is "obvious" to one man may well be obscure to another. Many of our greatest newspapers have in the past few years denounced the Democratic Party under Franklin D. Roosevelt for "obvious anti-democratic objectives" and the President has often been accused, as have many Presidents before him, of anti-democratic "practices." On the other hand, would a stockholder in a corporation given to obviously undemocratic practices be barred by this resolution, a stockholder in Girdler's Republic Steel, for instance?

The phrasing of the resolution is dangerous, its context is worse. The Civil Liberties Union was founded in 1920. The Soviet Union was established in 1917, and with it the "dictatorship of the proletariat." We are told that Communists are to be barred from office or employment in the Civil Liberties Union because, while fighting for civil liberties in America, they accept their suppression in Soviet Russia. Why, then, did the Civil Liberties Union wait until 1940 before seeking to bar them?

"The answer," the Civil Liberties Union said in a letter to its friends, "is to be found in the entirely new direction of the Communist movement since the Nazi-Soviet pact." But civil liberties within the Soviet Union were no different before the pact than after. One could not print an opposition paper in Moscow in August, 1939, before the pact, or after it, in September, 1939. In any case, what does the pact have to do with American civil liberties?

Could it be that the majority of the National Committee and the Board of Directors of the Civil Liberties Union is taking sides in the developing European conflict? Is their real objection an objection to the position of the Soviet Union in that conflict? Has that question anything to do with the need for defending civil liberties in America?

The phrasing of the purge resolution is so wide as to make the Civil Liberties Union seem a fellow-traveler of the Dies Committee. Its context is such as to make it seem that the Civil Liberties Union has been unable to keep its head in the kind of crisis that is the greatest danger to civil liberties.

The Civil Liberties Union is too valuable an organization and too precious a symbol. We ask it to turn back from this far-reaching step away from its traditions. We call upon it to rescind the purge resolution. We urge it to confine itself—as in the past—to civil liberties at home and leave international politics to other organizations.

The Civil Liberties Union has often found it necessary to

mobilize public sentiment in order to defend civil liberties. Never before has it been necessary to mobilize public sentiment in order to defend civil liberties within the Civil Liberties Union.

The Civil Liberties Union was formed in 1920 to fight post-war hysteria. It would be a great pity if it were now to become the victim of pre-war hysteria.

CHARLES S. ASCHER, *Social Science Research Council*

JOHN T. BERNARD, *ex-Congressman from Minnesota*

FRANZ BOAS, *Professor Emeritus, Columbia University*

WILLIAM T. COCHRAN *of Baltimore*

HOWARD COSTIGAN, *Executive Director, Washington Commonwealth Federation*

THEODORE DREISER, *author*

HENRY PRATT FAIRCHILD, *Professor at New York University*

HENRY T. HUNT, *U. S. Department of Interior*

GARDNER JACKSON, *legislative counsel of Labor's Non-Partisan League*

ROBERT MORSS LOVETT, *Secretary of the Virgin Islands*

ROBERT S. LYND, *Professor at Columbia University*

CAREY MCWILLIAMS, *California Commissioner of Immigration and Housing*

REV. A. T. MOLLEGAN, *Alexandria Theological Seminary*

I. F. STONE, *Associate Editor of* The Nation

MAXWELL S. STEWART, *Associate Editor of* The Nation

C. FAYETTE TAYLOR, *Professor at the Massachusetts Institute of Technology*

JAMES WECHSLER, *Assistant Editor of* The Nation

THE CONSTITUTION AND BY-LAWS OF THE COMMUNIST PARTY OF THE UNITED STATES OF AMERICA

This Constitution was unanimously adopted by the Tenth National Convention of the Communist Party of the U.S.A., in New York, May 27 to 31, 1938, after two months of pre-Convention discussion in every Branch of the Party. In its final form it was subsequently ratified by the Party membership after discussion in the Branches of the Party.

CONSTITUTION

PREAMBLE

The Communist Party of the United States of America is a working class political party carrying forward today the traditions of Jefferson, Paine, Jackson, and Lincoln, and of the Declaration of Independence; it upholds the achievements of democracy, the right of "life, liberty, and the pursuit of happiness," and defends the United States Constitution against its reactionary enemies who would destroy democracy and all popular liberties; it is devoted to defense of the immediate interests of workers, farmers, and all toilers against capitalist exploitation, and to preparation of the working class for its historic mission to unite and lead the American people to extend these democratic principles to their necessary and logical conclusions:

By establishing common ownership of the national economy, through a government of the people, by the people, and for the people; the abolition of all exploitation of man by man, nation by nation, and race by race, and thereby the abolition of class divisions in society; that is, by the establishment of socialism, according to the scientific principles enunciated by the greatest teachers of mankind, Marx, Engels, Lenin, and Stalin, embodied in the Communist International; and the free cooperation of the American people with those of other lands, striving toward a world without oppression and war, a world brotherhood of man.

To this end, the Communist Party of the United States of America establishes the basic laws of its organization in the following Constitution.

ARTICLE I

Name

The name of this organization shall be the COMMUNIST PARTY OF THE UNITED STATES OF AMERICA.

ARTICLE II

Emblem

The emblem of the Party shall be the crossed hammer and sickle, representing the unity of worker and farmer, with a circular inscription having at the top "Communist Party of the U.S.A." and in the lower part "Affiliated to the Communist International."

ARTICLE III

Membership

Section 1. Any person, eighteen years of age or more, regardless of race, sex, color, religious belief, or nationality, who is a citizen or who declares his intention of becoming a citizen of the United States, and whose loyalty to the working class is unquestioned, shall be eligible for membership.

Section 2. A Party member is one who accepts the Party program, attends the regular meetings of the membership Branch of his place of work or of his territory or trade, who pays dues regularly and is active in Party work.

Section 3. An applicant for membership shall sign an application card which shall be endorsed by at least two members of the Communist Party. Applications are subject to discussion and decision by the basic organization of the Party (shop, industrial, neighborhood Branch) to which the application is presented. After the applicant is accepted by a majority vote of the membership of the Branch present at a regular meeting he shall publicly pledge as follows:

> "I pledge firm loyalty to the best interests of the working class and full devotion to all progressive movements of the people. I pledge to work actively for the preservation and extension of democracy and peace, for the defeat of fascism and all forms of national oppression, for equal rights to the Negro people and for the establishment of socialism. For this purpose, I solemnly pledge to remain true to the principles of the Communist Party, to maintain its unity of purpose and action, and to work to the best of my ability to fulfil its program."

Section 4. There shall be no members-at-large without special permission of the National or State Committee.

Section 5. Party members two months in arrears in payment of dues cease to be members of the Party in good standing, and must be informed thereof.

Section 6. Members who are four months in arrears shall be stricken from the Party rolls. Every member three months in arrears shall be officially informed of this provision, and a personal effort shall be made to bring such member into good standing. However, if a member who for these reasons has been stricken from the rolls applies for readmission within six months, he may, on the approval of the next higher Party committee, be permitted to pay up his back dues and keep his standing as an old member.

ARTICLE IV

Initiation and Dues

Section 1. The initiation fee for an employed person shall be 50 cents and for an unemployed person 10 cents.

Section 2. Dues shall be paid every month according to rates fixed by the National Party Convention.

Section 3. The income from dues shall be distributed to the various Party organizations as follows:

a. 25 per cent to the Branch.
b. 35 per cent to the National Office.
c. The remaining 40 per cent shall be distributed among the respective State, County, City and Section Organizations in accordance with decisions of the State Conventions.

Section 4. Fifty per cent of the initiation fee shall be sent to the National Committee and 50 per cent shall remain with the State Organization.

ARTICLE V

International Solidarity and Assessment

Section 1. Every four months, all members of the Party shall pay an assessment equal to the average dues payment per month for the previous four months, for an International Solidarity Fund. This money shall be used by the National Committee exclusively to aid our brother Communist Parties in other countries suffering from fascist and military reaction.

Section 2. All local or district assessments are prohibited, except by special permission of the National Committee. Special assessments may be levied by the National Convention or the National Committee. No member shall be considered in good standing unless he purchases stamps for such special assessments.

Rights and Duties of Members

Section 1. The Communist Party of the U.S.A. upholds the democratic achievements of the American people. It opposes with all its power any clique, group, circle, faction or party which conspires or acts to subvert, undermine, weaken or overthrow any or all institutions of American democracy whereby the majority of the American people have obtained power to determine their own destiny in any degree. The Communist Party of the U.S.A., standing unqualifiedly for the right of the majority to direct the destinies of our country, will fight with all its strength against any and every effort, whether it comes from abroad or from within, to impose upon our people the arbitrary will of any selfish minority group or party or clique or conspiracy.

Section 2. Every member of the Party who is in good standing has not only the right, but the duty, to participate in the making of the policies of the Party and in the election of its leading committees, in a manner provided for in the Constitution.

Section 3. In matters of state or local nature, the Party organizations have the right to exercise full initiative and to make decisions within the limits of the general policies and decisions of the Party.

Section 4. After thorough discussion, the majority vote decides the policy of the Party, and the minority is duty-bound to carry out the decision.

Section 5. Party members disagreeing with any decision of a Party organization or committee have the right to appeal that decision to the next higher body, and may carry the appeal to the highest bodies of the Communist Party of the U.S.A., its National Committee and the National Convention. Decisions of the National Convention are final. While the appeal is pending, the decision must nevertheless be carried out by every member of the Party.

Section 6. In pre-Convention periods, individual Party members and delegates to the Convention shall have unrestricted right of discussion on any question of Party policy and tactics and the work and future composition of the leading committees.

Section 7. The decisions of the Convention shall be final and every Party member and Party organization shall be duty-bound to recognize the authority of the Convention decisions and the leadership elected by it.

Section 8. All Party members in mass organizations (trade unions, farm and fraternal organizations, etc.), shall cooperate to promote and strengthen the given organization and shall abide by the democratic decisions of these organizations.

Section 9. It shall be the duty of Party members to explain the mass policies of the Party and the principles of socialism.

Section 10. All Party members who are eligible shall be required to belong to their respective trade unions.

Section 11. All officers and leading committees of the Party from the Branch Executive Committee up to the highest committees are elected either directly by the membership or through their elected delegates. Every committee must report regularly on its activities to its Party organization.

Section 12. Any Party officer may be removed at any time from his position by a majority vote of the body which elected him, or by the body to which he is responsible, with the approval of the National Committee.

Section 13. Requests for release of a Party member from responsible posts may be granted only by the Party organization which elected him, or to which he is responsible, in consultation with the next higher committee.

Section 14. No Party member shall have personal or political relationship with confirmed Trotskyites, Lovestoneites, or other known enemies of the Party and of the working class.

Section 15. All Party members eligible shall register and vote in the elections for all public offices.

ARTICLE VII

Structure of the Party

Section 1. The basic organizations of the Communist Party of the U.S.A. are the shop, industrial and territorial Branches.

The Executive Committee of the Branch shall be elected once a year by the membership.

Section 2. The Section Organization shall comprise all Branches in a given territory of the city or state. The Section territory shall be defined by the higher Party committee and shall cover one or more complete political divisions of the city or state.

The highest body of the Section Organization is the Section Convention, or special annual Council meeting, called for the election of officers, which shall convene every year. The Section Convention or special Council meeting discusses and decides on policy and elects delegates to the higher Convention.

Between Section Conventions, the highest Party body in the Section Organization is the Section Council, composed of delegates elected proportionately from each Branch for a period of one year. Where no Section Council exists, the highest Party body is the Section Committee, elected by a majority vote of the Section Convention, which also elects the Section Organizer.

The Section Council or Section Committee may elect a Section Executive Committee which is responsible to the body that elected it. Non-members of the Section Council may be elected to the Executive Committee only with the approval of the next higher committee.

Section 3. In localities where there is more than one Section Organization, a City or County Council or Committee may be formed in accordance with the By-Laws.

Section 4. The State Organization shall comprise all Party organizations in one state.

The highest body of the State Organization is the State Convention, which shall convene every two years, and shall be composed of delegates elected by the Conventions of the subdivisions of the Party or Branches in the state. The delegates are elected on the basis of numerical strength.

A State Committee of regular and alternate members shall be elected at the State Convention with full power to carry out the decisions of the Convention and conduct the activities of the State Organization until the next State Convention.

The State Committee may elect from among its members an Executive Committee, which shall be responsible to the State Committee.

Special State Conventions may be called either by a majority vote of the State Committee, or upon written request of the Branches representing one-third of the membership of the state, with the approval of the National Committee.

Section 5. District Organizations may be established by the

National Committee, covering two or more states. In such cases the State Committees shall be under the jurisdiction of the District Committees, elected by and representing the Party organizations of the states composing these Districts. The rules of convening District Conventions and the election of leading committees shall be the same as those provided for the State Organization.

ARTICLE VIII

National Organization

Section 1. The supreme authority in the Communist Party of the U.S.A. is the National Convention. Regular National Conventions shall be held every two years. Only such a National Convention is authorized to make political and organizational decisions binding upon the entire Party and its membership, except as provided in Article VIII, Section 6.

Section 2. The National Convention shall be composed of delegates elected by the State and District Conventions. The delegates are elected on the basis of numerical strength of the State Organizations. The basis for representation shall be determined by the National Committee.

Section 3. For two months prior to the Convention, discussions shall take place in all Party organizations on the main resolutions and problems coming before the Convention. During this discussion all Party organizations have the right and duty to adopt resolutions and amendments to the Draft Resolutions of the National Committee for consideration at the Convention.

Section 4. The National Convention elects the National Committee, a National Chairman and General Secretary by majority vote. The National Committee shall be composed of regular and alternate members. The alternate members shall have voice but no vote.

Section 5. The size of the National Committee shall be decided upon by each National Convention of the Party. Members of the National Committee must have been active members of the Party for at least three years.

Section 6. The National Committee is the highest authority of the Party between National Conventions, and is responsible for

200

enforcing the Constitution and securing the execution of the general policies adopted by the democratically elected delegates in the National Convention assembled. The National Committee represents the Party as a whole, and has the right to make decisions with full authority on any problem facing the Party between Conventions. The National Committee organizes and supervises its various departments and committees; conducts all the political and organizational work of the Party; appoints or removes the editors of its press, who work under its leadership and control; organizes and guides all undertakings of importance for the entire Party; distributes the Party forces and controls the central treasury. The National Committee, by majority vote of its members, may call special State or National Conventions. The National Committee shall submit a certified, audited financial report to each National Convention.

Section 7. The National Committee elects from among its members a Political Committee and such additional secretaries and such departments and committees as may be considered necessary for most efficient work. The Political Committee is charged with the responsibility of carrying out the decisions and the work of the National Committee between its full sessions. It is responsible for all its decisions to the National Committee. The size of the Political Committee shall be decided upon by majority vote of the National Committee.

Members of the Political Committee and editors of the central Party organs must have been active members of the Party for not less than five years.

The National Committee shall meet at least once in four months.

The Political Committee of the National Committee shall meet weekly.

The National Committee may, when it deems it necessary, call Party Conferences. The National Committee shall decide the basis of attendance at such Conferences. Such Conferences shall be consultative bodies auxiliary to the National Committee.

ARTICLE IX

National Control Commission

Section 1. For the purpose of maintaining and strengthening Party unity and discipline, and of supervising the audits of the financial books and records of the National Committee of the Party and its enterprises, the National Committee elects a National Control Commission, consisting of the most exemplary Party members, each of whom shall have been an active Party member for at least five years. The size of the National Control Commission shall be determined by the National Committee.

Section 2. On various disciplinary cases, such as those concerning violations of Party unity, discipline or ethics, or concerning lack of class vigilance and Communist firmness in facing the class enemy, or concerning spies, swindlers, double-dealers and other agents of the class enemy—the National Control Commission shall be charged with making investigations and decisions, either on appeals against the decisions of lower Party bodies, or on cases which are referred to it by the National Committee, or on cases which the National Control Commission itself deems necessary to take up directly.

Section 3. The decisions of the National Control Commission shall go into effect as soon as their acceptance by the National Committee or its Political Committee is assured.

Section 4. Members of the National Control Commission shall have the right to participate in the sessions of the National Committee with voice but no vote.

Section 5. Meetings of the National Control Commission shall take place at least once every month.

ARTICLE X

Disciplinary Procedure

Section 1. Breaches of Party discipline by individual members, financial irregularities, as well as any conduct or action detrimental to the Party's prestige and influence among the working masses and harmful to the best interests of the Party, may be punished by censure, public censure, removal from responsible posts, and by expulsion from the Party. Breaches of discipline by Party Committees may be punished by removal of the Committee by the next higher Party Committee, which shall then conduct new elections.

Section 2. Charges against individual members may be made by any person—Party or non-Party—in writing, to the Branches of the Party or to any leading committee. The Party Branch shall have the right to decide on any disciplinary measure, including expulsion. Such action is subject to final approval by the State Committee.

Section 3. The Section, State, and National Committees and the National Control Commission have the right to hear and take disciplinary action against any individual member or organization under their jurisdiction.

Section 4. All parties concerned shall have the fullest right to appear, to bring witnesses and to testify before the Party organization. The member punished shall have the right to appeal any disciplinary decision to the higher committees up to the National Convention of the Party.

Section 5. Party members found to be strikebreakers, degenerates, habitual drunkards, betrayers of Party confidence, provocateurs, advocates of terrorism and violence as a method of Party procedure, or members whose actions are detrimental to the Party and the working class, shall be summarily dismissed from positions of responsibility, expelled from the Party and exposed before the general public.

ARTICLE XI

Affiliation

The Communist Party of the U.S.A. is affiliated with its fraternal Communist Parties of other lands through the Communist International and participates in International Congresses, through its National Committee. Resolutions and decisions of International Congresses shall be considered and acted upon by the supreme authority of the Communist Party of the U.S.A., the National Convention, or between Conventions, by the National Committee.

ARTICLE XII

Amending the Constitution

Section 1. This Constitution and By-Laws may be amended as follows: (a) by decision of a majority of the voting delegates present at the National Convention, provided the proposed amendment has been published in the Party press or Discussion Bulletins of the National Committee at least thirty days prior to the Convention; (b) by the National Committee for the purpose of complying with any law of any state or of the United States or whenever any provisions of this Constitution and By-Laws conflict with any such law. Such amendments made by the National Committee shall be published in the Party press or Discussion Bulletins of the National Committee and shall remain in full force and effect until acted upon by the National Convention.

Section 2. Any amendment submitted by a State Committee or State Convention within the time provided for shall be printed in the Party press.

ARTICLE XIII

By-Laws

Section 1. By-Laws shall be adopted, based on this Constitution, for the purpose of establishing uniform rules and procedure for the proper functioning of the Party organizations. By-Laws may be adopted or changed by majority vote of the National Convention, or between Conventions by majority vote of the National Committee.

Section 2. State By-Laws not in conflict with the National Constitution and By-Laws may be adopted or changed by majority vote of the State Convention or, between Conventions, by majority vote of the State Committee.

ARTICLE XIV

Charters

The National Committee shall issue Charters to State or District Organizations and at the request of the respective State Organizations, to County and City Organizations, defining the territory over which they have jurisdiction and authority.

RULES AND BY-LAWS

The following are the Rules and By-Laws adopted by the Communist Party of the United States of America, in accordance with its Constitution, for the purpose of carrying out the principles, rights and duties as established in the Constitution in a uniform manner in all Party organizations.

Basic Organizations

The basic organizations of the Communist Party of the U.S.A. are the shop, territorial and industrial Branches. A shop Branch consists of those Party members who are employed in the same place of employment. Shop Branches shall be organized in every factory, shop, mine, ship, dock, office, etc., where there is a sufficient number of Party members, but no less than seven.

A territorial Branch consists of members of the Party living in the same neighborhood or territory. Territorial Branches shall be organized on the basis of the political division of the city or town (assembly district, ward, precinct, election district, town or township, etc.).

Industrial Branches may be organized and shall consist of Party members employed in the same trade or industry and shall be composed of those Party members who are employed in places where shop Branches have not yet been formed. Shop Branches shall be organized wherever possible.

Every Branch of the Party shall elect an Executive Committee, which shall consist of at least the following officers: chairman, treasurer, educational director, membership director. There may be a recording secretary whose functions may be filled by one of the other officers. The size of the Executive Committee shall be determined by the size of the Branch, but shall not be less than four.

The Executive Committee has the duty of preparing the agenda and proposals for the membership meeting, administering and executing the decisions of the membership and the higher

Party committee, and, between Branch meetings, of making decisions concerning matters which require immediate action. The Executive Committee of the Branch shall report regularly on its work, which shall be subject to review and action by the membership.

Regular election of Branch officers shall take place yearly, but not more than twice a year. All officers shall be elected by majority vote of the membership at a specially designated meeting of which the whole membership shall be notified. Officers may be replaced by majority vote of the Branch membership at any time, with the approval of the higher Party committee.

Financial statements shall be submitted to the Branch by the Executive Committee at least quarterly.

The order of business at the Branch meeting shall include the following:

1. Reading of minutes of previous meeting;
2. Dues payments and initiation of new members;
3. Report of Executive Committee:
   a. Check-up on decisions (old business);
   b. Assignments and tasks, reports on communications, literature and press (new business);
4. Good and welfare;
5. Regular educational discussion (educational discussion may be moved to any point on the order of business).

Collections within Party organizations in a given territory may be made only with the approval of the next higher body.

One-third of the Branch membership shall constitute a quorum.

Branches shall meet at least once every two weeks.

Section Organizations

Delegates to the Section Convention or Council shall be elected by all Branches in proportion to their membership. The basis of representation shall be decided upon by the Section Committee in consultation with the higher Party Committee.

Any delegate to the Section Council may be recalled by a

majority vote of his Branch. The Section Council meets regularly once a month.

The Section Council shall make a report at least once in three months to the general membership meeting of the Section. All Party members residing in the territory may be invited to these meetings.

The Section Council shall submit financial reports to the Branches and to the higher Party Committee at least once in three months.

City or County Organizations

In cities where there is more than one Section Organization, a City Council may be formed by the election of delegates either from the Section Councils or directly from the Branches. The role of this form of organization is to coordinate and guide the work on a citywide scale, and actively participate in or supervise Party activity in all public elections and civic affairs within its territory.

The City Council elects from among its members a City Executive Committee with the same rights and duties on a citywide scale as the Section Executive Committee has on a Sectionwide scale.

The State Committee may form County Councils with the same rights and duties on a county scale as the City Council has on a city scale.

The structure of the County Council shall be the same as of the City Council.

State or District Organizations

For two months prior to the State Convention, discussion shall take place in all Party organizations on the main resolutions and problems coming before the Convention. During this discussion, all Party organizations have the right and duty to adopt resolutions and amendments to the Draft Resolutions of the State Committee, for consideration at the Convention.

Only members who are at least two years in the Party shall be eligible for elections to the State Committee. Exceptions may be made only by State or National Conventions. The size of the State Committee shall be decided upon by the Convention, in consultation with the National Committee.

The State Committee shall meet at least once every two months. It shall elect from among its members an Executive Committee to function with full power, which shall be responsible to the State Committee.

The State Committee, by a majority vote of its members, may replace any regular member who is unable to serve because of sickness or other assignment, or who is removed from office. New regular members shall be chosen from among the alternate members of the State Committee.

An auditing committee, elected by the State Committee, shall examine the books of the State Financial Secretary once every month. A Certified Public Accountant shall audit these books at least once a year, and his report shall be presented to the State Committee and Conventions.

Special State Conventions may be called by a majority vote of the State Committee, or by the National Committee.

Upon the written request of Branches representing one-third of the membership of the State Organization, the State Committee shall call a special State Convention.

The call for a special Convention shall be subject to the approval of the National Committee.

The State Committee shall have the power to establish an official organ with the approval of the National Committee.

The State Committee shall conduct or supervise Party activity in all public elections and statewide public affairs within the state.

In states having more than one thousand members, the State Committee shall appoint a Disciplinary Committee with the task of hearing disciplinary cases, and reporting its findings and recommendations to the State Committee. In states with less than one thousand members, a Committee may be appointed if it is considered necessary.

The rules governing the organization and functioning of District Organizations shall be the same as those provided for the State Organizations.

Qualifications for Delegates to Conventions

Delegates to the State Conventions must be in good standing and have been members of the Party for at least one year.

Delegates to the National Convention must be in good standing and have been members of the Party for at least two years.

In special cases, the latter qualification (length of time in Party) may be waived, but only with the approval of the leading committee involved (National Committee for the National Convention, State Committee for the State Convention).

Membership

It is within the provision of Article III, Section 1 of the Constitution that the following are eligible to membership in the Communist Party:

a. Persons who, by some present unjust and undemocratic laws, are excluded from citizenship and disbarred from legally declaring their intentions of becoming citizens;
b. Students and others temporarily residing in the country;
c. All persons coming from countries contiguous to the United States, engaged in migratory work, and temporarily in the country.

Rate of Dues

Dues shall be paid every month according to the following rates:

a. Housewives, unemployed, and all members earning up to $47.00 a month, shall pay 10 cents a month.
b. All members earning from $47.01 to $80.00 a month inclusive shall pay 25 cents a month.
c. All members earning from $80.01 to $112.00 a month inclusive shall pay 50 cents a month.
d. All members earning from $112.01 to $160.00 a month inclusive shall pay $1.00 a month.

e. Members earning more than $160.00 per month shall pay, besides the regular $1.00 dues, additional dues at the rate of 50 cents for each additional $10.00 or fraction thereof.

All dues payments must be acknowledged in the membership book by dues stamps issued by the National Committee.

Transfers and Leaves of Absence

Members who move from one neighborhood, shop or industry to another and have to go from one Branch to another, shall obtain transfers from their Branches. No member shall be accepted by the new Branch without a properly filled out transfer card. Before receiving transfers, members shall be in good standing and have paid up all other financial obligations to their Branches. If a member transfers from one Section or City Organization to another, a duplicate transfer card shall be transmitted through the State or District Committee. If a member transfers from one State or District to another, this shall be recorded in the membership book, and a duplicate transfer card shall be sent through the National Committee.

No member has the right to take a leave of absence without the permission of his Branch. Leaves of absence not exceeding one month may be granted by the Branch. An extended leave of absence, upon the recommendation of the Branch, shall be acted upon by the next higher committee of the Party. Before a leave of absence is given the member shall pay up dues, and settle his financial obligations up to and including the end of the leave of absence period.

Readmittance

Expelled members applying for readmittance must submit a written statement and their applications may not be finally acted upon except with the approval of the National Control Commission.

Former members whose membership has lapsed must submit a written statement on application for readmission, to be finally acted upon by the respective State Committees.

LETTER OF RESIGNATION, MARCH 2, 1940, FROM DR. HARRY F. WARD, CHAIRMAN OF A.C.L.U. BOARD OF DIRECTORS, 1920–1940

I have received and carefully considered the Resolution concerning qualifications for service on the governing bodies and staff of the Union passed by the National Committee and the Board on February 5.

Contrary to the "Statement to the Press" authorized by the Board on the same date which says that "the resolution does not, however, change the fundamental policy of the Union over the twenty years of its existence," I find that the resolution does inaugurate a new policy.

It sets up a "test of consistency in the defense of civil liberties in all aspects and all places." It declares "that consistency is inevitably compromised by persons who champion civil liberties in the United States and yet who justify or tolerate the denial of civil liberties by dictatorships abroad." During its entire existence the Union has rigidly excluded from its consideration civil liberties issues outside the United States. It has several times refused invitations to international collaboration in its field of work. The Resolution of February 5 now sets up as a test for membership in its Board and National Committee the attitude of persons toward the actions and policies of foreign governments.

The authorized "Statement to the Press" acknowledges that the resolution "appears to set up a test of opinion." I find that it actually does set up tests of opinion. Its provisions cannot be carried out except by an examination of opinions. How else can it be determined whether a person is justifying or tolerating "the denial of civil liberties by dictatorships abroad"? The resolution disqualifies for membership in the governing bodies of the Union anyone "who is a member of any political organization which supports totalitarian dictatorship in any country, or who by his public declarations indicates his support of such a principle." What constitutes "totalitarian dictatorship" in different countries, at different times, is a question of political opinion on which there is a strong difference. In the light of this fact, the determination of what "public declarations" indicate support of the principle of "totalitarian dictatorship" becomes a censorship of the opinions of some by the opinions of others.

In thus penalizing opinions, the Union is doing in its own sphere what it has always opposed the government for doing in law or administration. The essence of civil liberties is opposition to all attempts to enforce political orthodoxy. Yet by this resolution the Civil Liberties Union is attempting to create an orthodoxy in civil liberties, and stranger still, an orthodoxy in political judgment upon events outside the United States, in situations of differing degrees of democratic development. The majority of the Board and of the National Committee, acting under the pressure of wartime public opinion, tells the minority to conform to its views or get out. What kind of civil liberties is this? It is certainly not the kind which has been proclaimed in all our printed matter from the beginning.

Furthermore, when the Union disqualifies for membership in its governing bodies any person "who is a member of any political organization which supports totalitarian dictatorship in any country" it is using the principle of guilt by association which it has always opposed when the government has sought to enforce it. At this point the resolution becomes concrete only in relation to the Communist Party. The inclusion of other organizations is irrelevant window-dressing. In view of the fact that in all of our discussions over this issue I have heard no one challenge the record in defense of civil liberties of the one Communist member of the Board (a charter member of the Union), I cannot agree that mere membership in the Communist Party disqualifies one for service on the governing bodies of the Union.

Neither can I accept the affirmation of the authorized "Statement to the Press" that, "The present resolution merely states what has been always the unwritten policy of the Union in elections or appointments." That is no more accurate than the following assertion that, "Its sole effect will be to apply that policy to present membership," when obviously future membership is also determined by it. If the policy of the resolution had been the "unwritten policy of the Union" when two Board members, at different times, became members of the Communist Party, the Board would have been in duty bound to point out that their resignations were in order. The further fact that one of these persons asked the Board whether joining the Communist Party made continuance on the Board undesirable, and was answered "No," proves that the policy of the resolution was not then the "unwritten policy of the Union."

Throughout its existence, aside from those personal qualifications which all reputable organizations require, the Union has had only one test in selecting the members of its Board and National Committee. That test has been their attitude toward the Bill of Rights and their record in defense of it. In my judgment it needs no other test now.

It is also my judgment that when the majority of the National Committee and of the Board, acting, according to the authorized "Statement to the Press," under "the increasing tension which has resulted everywhere from the direction of the Communist international movement since the Soviet-Nazi pact," adopted the further tests set forth in the Resolution of February 5, they surrendered positions vital to the defense of civil liberties, positions whose defense under constant attack is the honorable record of the Union. I cannot go with them in this surrender. The Civil Liberties Union which did this is not the Civil Liberties Union with which I have been glad to work for twenty years. Reluctant as I am to sever this long association, I am compelled by the policy that has been adopted to withdraw from the Board and from membership in the Union.

PROTEST TO THE A.C.L.U. NATIONAL COMMITTEE AND BOARD OF DIRECTORS BY THREE MEMBERS OF THE NATIONAL COMMITTEE, MARCH 21, 1940

The undersigned hereby ask you for reconsideration and reversal of the action taken on February 5, establishing, by general legislation, conditions of eligibility for office-holding in the Union. We are convinced that those actions, taken under the stress of controversy, are false to the principles of the Union.

The Resolution of February 5 has to do with the relation of candidates for office to "totalitarian dictatorships in any country." Inasmuch as the actual problem in the National Board has arisen only in connection with relation to Russia and to the Communist Party we limit our argument to the issue in that form.

The wording of paragraph three of the Resolution of February 5 sets up qualifications for office-holding which rule out any member of the Communist Party. But the resolution goes farther. When considered in connection with Paragraph 2, and with the circumstances attending the introduction and adoption of the resolution, the meaning of the resolution as a whole is broadened to exclude those "who justify or tolerate the denial of civil liberties by dictatorships abroad." As against this, we can easily conceive of men and women who are devoted champions of civil liberties and who yet retain a hope that Russia will in time fulfil the promises of the Constitution of 1936 and free itself of the tyranny and terrorism that have appalled liberals throughout the world.

The resolution seems, when taken as a whole, to go so far as to exclude from office in the Union those who "tolerate" dictatorship abroad. It is possible, without straining the meaning of words, to interpret this as excluding all those who do not favor an active interference in the internal affairs of a distant country of which our knowledge is imperfect and in which—shocking as the excesses of governmental authority have been—substantial progress seems to have been made in checking the arbitrary power over the lives of men that had been there, and is still in politically democratic countries, inherent in the private ownership and control of natural resources and machinery.

Some American liberals decided at the outset of the Bolshevist Revolution, from the moment when the Constituent Assembly was dissolved, that no good would come of it. Others made allowances for a largely illiterate nation prostrated by war and economic collapse and hoped that the dictatorship would be of short duration. Others abandoned all sympathy and hope for the Bolshevist experiment at the time of the purges. And since the Russian-Nazi pact many other American liberals who up to the time had clung to their hope for Russia have abandoned that hope.

It is not for the governing committee of an organization existing solely for the defense of freedom of thought and expression to require that any of our colleagues should think as we do in relation to the Russian experiment. The sole test for us is our sincere devotion to the American Bill of Rights and the principles underlying it, and that devotion is to be tested, not by adherence to any such sweeping and ambiguous declaration as that of February 5, but by the attitude of each individual officer or committeeman to civil liberties in the United States. Even in this field there is room for honest differences of opinion on specific cases.

The Minutes of February 5, item 7, seem to indicate that the National Committee and the National Board had determined to go even further. The vote then taken seemed to exclude from office one other class of members, viz: those who oppose the passing of the resolution. In accordance with that action, officers were to be re-elected only "on condition that they approve in principle the resolution adopted." We know, from our own experience, that such candidates were officially asked whether or not they did so approve, the implication being that, if not, they would not be re-elected. We learn from later minutes, however, that the Board is still uncertain as to the exact wording and intention of the action taken, and even of its constitutionality. Under the circumstances we can only express the hope that the decision of the Committee and Board will not, as first appeared, have the effect of an expulsion of a minority group by a victorious majority.

The explanations given by the majority in defense of its action stress very strongly the sharp differences of opinion which have arisen in the Board and which have interfered with its efficiency. There seems little doubt of the seriousness of the situation. We are, however, left almost wholly in the dark as to what the specific differences are and in what specific forms the minority group is accused of hindering the work of the Board.

It seems very probable, in the light of our limited knowledge, that bad feeling between factions, with the factor of personalities playing its part, is at the bottom of this deplorable situation. And we cannot escape the conclusion that one faction of the Committee and the Board have taken advantage of the current intense feeling against Communists and Communist sympathizers to purge a minority with whom they have for a long time conducted a bitter feud.

We should protest the action of February 5 if only because of its timing. This, in our opinion, could not have been worse. If Communists or Communist sympathizers can obstruct the work of the Committee, it would seem to us that their power for mischief must have been far greater a few years or even a few months ago, when the Communist cause was far more popular and even enjoyed a vogue among liberal intellectuals, and that that power must now be reduced to the minimum. We cannot escape the conclusion that the Union by this action has yielded to the same wave of intolerance that is manifested by the general reaction throughout the country and has thereby given aid and comfort to forces and tendencies that threaten all the progress we have made in recent years, not least in the field of civil liberties.

In all discussions of this matter the point should be kept clear that the brunt of the attack of the majority is directed, not against Communists, but against Communist sympathizers. For many years there has been only one Communist member on the Board and it is very certain that she is not the cause of all this desperate trouble. With respect to the others, the non-Communist minority, we would hold as strongly as any one can possibly do, that if in any concrete or verifiable way, they have shown disloyalty to the purpose of the Union, they should be debarred from office. But, in that case, exclusion should be based, not on the ground of their relation to Russia or, it may be, to Germany or Spain or Italy or others of like character, but on the ground of their disloyalty to the Union itself.

As against the new policy we ask for a return to the traditional procedure of the Union. The members of the National Board must learn to deal with each other and with their disputes by the methods of rational, free discussion. If they cannot do that, it is idle for them to recommend the methods of democracy to others. In saying this we protest that no one should be elected to office in the Union, no one should be continued in office in the Union, unless he is heartily and unreservedly loyal to the spirit of the Bill of Rights. But the question of loyalty should be determined, not by general tests of opinion on questions more or less unrelated to the work of the Union, but upon the careful scrutiny, case by case, of the qualities and attitudes of the candidate himself. On two occasions in the past the Union has asked the withdrawal of a prominent member on the ground that his opinions or actions were no longer consistent with the Bill of Rights. That is the only honest and direct way of dealing with such a situation. It is the only way which is consistent with the purposes of the Union itself. We are convinced that the majority of the National Committee and of the Board has been led by the stress of controversy, into the adoption of a false and unwise policy. We ask therefore for a reversal of the action.

Sincerely yours,
ALEXANDER MEIKLEJOHN
EDWARD L. PARSONS
GEORGE P. WEST

San Francisco

PROTEST BY A. F. WHITNEY, PRESIDENT OF THE BROTHERHOOD OF RAILROAD TRAINMEN AND A MEMBER OF THE NATIONAL COMMITTEE OF THE A.C.L.U.

Brotherhood of Railroad Trainmen
Cleveland, Ohio
August 16, 1940

Mr. Roger Baldwin, Director
American Civil Liberties Union
31 Union Square West
New York, New York

Dear Mr. Baldwin:

This will acknowledge receipt of your letter of August 2nd, in which you ask me to vote on the action of the Board of Directors of the American Civil Liberties Union in the case involving Miss Elizabeth Gurley Flynn. I attach hereto my ballot in this case and please note that I have voted to disapprove the action of the Board of Directors on May 7th in the Elizabeth Gurley Flynn case.* Permit me to state my reasons for this action.

I am prompted by no consideration of personal feelings for Miss Flynn. I do not even know her. Neither am I prompted by any regard for the Communist Party. I am, however, deeply concerned about the principles involved in this case. With Lincoln, I hate the principle of qualifying liberty, for, in the words of Lin-

---

* Mr. Whitney was listed by the A.C.L.U. as not voting, owing to the fact that his ballot was not returned to the national office before the deadline for counting the vote.—Ed.

coln, "it deprives our Republic of its just influence in the world, enables the enemies of free institutions everywhere to taunt us as hypocrites, causes the real friends of freedom to doubt our sincerity and especially because it forces so many good men among ourselves into an open war with the very fundamentals of civil liberty, denying the good faith of the Declaration of Independence and insisting that there is no right principle of action but self-interest." I am also reminded of Lincoln's timely warning when, in the Lincoln-Douglas debates, he declared:

> "When you have enslaved any of your fellow-beings, dehumanized them, denied them all claim to the dignity of manhood, placed them among the beasts, among the damned, are you quite sure that the demon you have thus created will not turn and rend you? When you start qualifying liberty, watch out for the consequences to you."

In determining whether the majority of the Board of Directors of the A.C.L.U. have created a monster which might some day turn and rend them, let me briefly state the facts as I understand them.

Miss Flynn was a charter member of the A.C.L.U. and had served as a member of the National Committee since 1920. She joined the Communist Party in 1937 and was unanimously re-elected to the Board of Directors of the A.C.L.U. in 1939, for a three-year term. According to the transcript of record in the case and according to "A Statement to Members and Friends of the American Civil Liberties Union," dated May, 1940, it seems that one Adolf Hitler, of the German Reich, entered into a compact with Soviet Russia and out of that arose the principal basis for the action against Miss Flynn. Apparently Hitler's crusade to save the world from "Communism"—momentarily comp[r]omised by his treaty with Russia—has been taken up by the American Civil Liberties Union, in violation of one of its fundamental precepts, namely:

> "The Union does not engage in political controversy. It takes no position on any political or economic issue or system. . . . It is wholly unconcerned with movements abroad or with foreign governments."

A reading of the transcript of the record of the alleged trial of Miss Flynn removes any doubt that the case of Elizabeth Gurley Flynn is a deep venture into political inquiry and a wide departure from the principle of civil liberties. There is not a scintilla of evidence indicating that Miss Flynn was or ever has been disloyal to the fundamental principles of the American Civil Liberties Union. No one ventured to attack her loyalty to the principles embraced by the American Civil Liberties Union. And even if she had been so attacked, let me point out that the very persons who sat in judgment on her were the ones who had previously formed an opinion as to her "guilt," and three of them were authors of the charges brought against her. The transcript plainly reveals to me that the "hearing" was more in the nature of a political convention or a Star Chamber proceeding than a true inquiry into the guilt or innocence of the accused.

The resolution and opinions of the majority of the Board of Directors might be used in a campaign for re-election of Miss Flynn, but certainly it is not even recited that there is anything in the Constitution or By-Laws of the American Civil Liberties Union that would justify opinions regarding "propriety" being made the basis of expulsion of an officer or member of the Union. One need not be a lawyer to read the transcript of the record in Miss Flynn's case and come to the conclusion that the same results might well have been reached, whatever Miss Flynn might have been charged with. If it is contended that the resolution of the Board of Directors was the legal basis on which Miss Flynn was removed, then let it be recorded that in this case the law-makers were the judges also, and three of the judges were authors of the indictment. I submit that the first and foremost duty of the American Civil Liberties Union is to establish some democratic machinery within its own organization, by which the democratic rights and the *civil liberties* of the officers and membership may be protected. It may be, as stated in the pamphlet of May, 1940, that "there is no 'civil liberty' in being a member of any Board of Directors. . . ." However, where membership of twenty years' standing and the prestige and reputation of an individual is at stake, there is certainly involved a deep principle of civil liberties in the manner by which that record of service and loyalty is terminated and the long prestige and reputation is destroyed. Let me state that the answer to paragraph 17, on page 14 of the quoted statement, does not impress me as coming from an expert in civil liberties.

It seems to me that the majority of the Board of Directors convict themselves of having been moved by popular fancy and fleeting public opinion, generated by a war hysteria, when the same individuals who voted to remove Miss Flynn also unanimously voted to re-elect her two years after she had become a member of the Communist Party. Their only excuse for such conduct seems to be that Adolf Hitler signed a treaty with Soviet Russia. I hope I have not yet reached the point where the actions or policies of Adolf Hitler and Soviet Russia control my thinking. The fact that the majority of the Board of Directors is moved by popular fancy is well revealed by the statement on page 6 of the pamphlet of May, 1940, wherein it is said:

> "There is no question but that the Union has been greatly strengthened in public opinion by this action. The unanimous and strongly worded approval of newspapers in editorial comments throughout the country, is a clear revelation of this."

My only comment here is that newspaper editorial opinion is hardly an adequate test of the validity of the policies of the American Civil Liberties Union.

On page 10, of the May, 1940, statement, in answer to the question whether the resolution penalizes mere opinions in the absence of any acts, the action of the Board of Directors in expelling Miss Flynn is thus defended:

> "The Union must, of course, base its selection of governing committees and staff on the ground of opinion—namely, support of the principle of civil liberties."

I submit that this is an acceptable statement, but where in the transcript of record is there one scintilla of evidence to show that Miss Flynn's removal was based upon her "opinion"? On the contrary, the evidence seems to indicate that she has a record of many years of faithfulness and loyalty to the American Civil Liberties Union and the principles for which it stands and that she was removed only because she belonged to a certain group. May

221

we again say with Lincoln, beware lest the demon thus created turn and rend us, because some time we might belong to an unpopular group.

The record indicates that unfortunate name-calling and inept statements have been made by more than one member of the Board of Directors. Miss Flynn had been publicly attacked and claimed the right of free expression of opinion as a matter of self-defense. Name-calling on the part of certain other members of the Board did not have the justification of self-defense, yet the latter were not punished and the former was. Simple justice and fair play would again suggest that Miss Flynn was punished not because of what she said or did, but because she belonged to a certain group.

I cannot refrain from calling your attention to page 18 of the transcript, wherein a member of the Board of Directors lays down the ideal of "like-mindedness" as an essential to "a voluntary association of persons who presumably have one common interest—the preservation of civil liberties." Of course, if the majority of the Board of Directors of the A.C.L.U. aspire to "like-mindedness," then let me recommend the goose-step and the salute, which are very effective in achieving that end.

It is stated that in the darkest hours of the Revolutionary War, George Washington descended alone into the forest and knelt in silent prayer. There were atheists associated with George Washington in the Revolutionary War, and they might have been adverse to participation in prayer. But the divergent faiths and associations of our forefathers never led them to disrupt their loyalty to their great common cause, their successful defense of which makes possible the American Civil Liberties Union today. The transcript of record does not reveal a single opinion or act of Miss Flynn which militates against the supposed common cause of the American Civil Liberties Union. For all the record reveals, Miss Flynn might have joined the Communist Party for the specific purpose of persuading that group to become more conscious of the high ideals to which the American Civil Liberties Union is dedicated.

I express no opinion as to the personal fitness of Miss Flynn to serve on the Board of Directors of the American Civil Liberties Union. I am only protesting what I regard as Star Chamber proceedings and the conviction of an individual without evidence and

apparently without a̶n̶y̶ ̶_̶_̶_̶_̶_̶ ̶g̶a̶_̶_̶ ̶_̶_̶_̶ such procedure. I could concede that the political campaign against Miss
Flynn might be persuasive in an election, but I solemnly submit
that the political campaign which masquerades as a trial to determine the question of her expulsion is not only an assault upon the
fundamental principles of the American Civil Liberties Union,
but an affront to the basic principles of civil liberties and true
Americanism.

Since I do not have the addresses of the members of the
Board and National Committee of the Civil Liberties Union, I
request that copies of this letter, which I am forwarding under
separate cover, be furnished them, so that they may know the
reasons for my vote.

With best wishes, I am

Sincerely yours,

A. F. WHITNEY

President.

VOTE OF THE NATIONAL COMMITTEE OF THE A.C.L.U. RATIFYING THE EXPULSION OF ELIZABETH GURLEY FLYNN

IN FAVOR

Dr. Harry Elmer Barnes
Judge John Beardsley
Herbert S. Bigelow
Prof. Edwin M. Borchard
Van Wyck Brooks
Sherwood Eddy
Kate Crane Gartz
Dr. John A. Lapp
Mrs. Agnes Brown Leach
James H. Maurer
A. J. Muste
Dr. William Allan Neilson
Bishop Edward L. Parsons
William Pickens
Amos R. Pinchot
Prof. E. A. Ross
John Nevin Sayre
Joseph Schlossberg
Robert E. Sherwood
Rabbi Abba Hillel Silver
John F. Sinclair
Prof. Clarence R. Skinner
Oswald Garrison Villard
Mrs. Richard J. Walsh
Peter Witt
L. Hollingsworth Wood
Dr. Mary E. Woolley

OPPOSED

Bishop Edgar Blake
John S. Codman
Dean Lloyd K. Garrison
Charles H. Houston
Henry T. Hunt
Robert Morss Lovett
Dr. Alexander Meiklejohn
Dean Elbert Russell
Bishop William Scarlett
Prof. Vida D. Scudder
Helen Phelps Stokes
George P. West

NOT VOTING

Prof. Sophonisba Breckinridge
Dean Christian Gauss
Dr. Frank P. Graham
Powers Hapgood
Hubert C. Herring
Dr. Frank Kingdon
George W. Kirchwey
Prof. Harold D. Lasswell
William Draper Lewis
Bishop G. Bromley Oxnam
Jeannette Rankin
A. F. Whitney